THE MIDDLE-AGE

Peter Lambley, PhD, is a clinical ps
years experience in psychological medicine and psychotherapy.
He is the author of several books and a number of journal and
magazine articles on psychological and medical subjects.

By the same author

The Psychology of Apartheid
How to Survive Anorexia
The Psychology of Cancer
The Headache Book
Insomnia and Other Sleep Disorders

The
Middle-Aged Rebel

RESPONDING TO THE CHALLENGES
OF MIDLIFE
●
A DYNAMIC APPROACH

Peter Lambley

ELEMENT
Shaftesbury, Dorset ● Rockport, Massachusetts
Brisbane, Queensland

© Peter Lambley 1995

First published in Great Britain in 1995 by
Element Books Limited
Shaftesbury, Dorset SP7 8BP

Published in the USA in 1995 by
Element Books, Inc.
42 Broadway, Rockport, MA 01966

Published in Australia in 1995 by
Element Books Limited
for Jacaranda Wiley Limited
33 Park Road, Milton, Brisbane 4064

All rights reserved.
No part of this book may be reproduced or utilized
in any form or by any means, in writing
electronic or mechanical,
without prior permission
in writing from the Publisher.

Cover design by Max Fairbrother
Design by Roger Lightfoot
Typeset by Footnote Graphics, Warminster, Wilts.
Printed and bound in Great Britain by
Hartnolls Limited, Bodmin, Cornwall

British Library Cataloguing in Publication data available

Library of Congress Cataloging in Publication Data

Lambley, Peter.
The middle-aged rebel: responding to the challenges of
midlife–a dynamic approach/Peter Lambley.
p. cm.
Includes bibliographical references and index.
1. Middle age–United States. 2. Middle aged persons–United
States–Psychology.
I. Title
HQ1059.5.U5L34   1995
305. 24 4–dc20   95–14064 CIP
ISBN 1–85230–644–0

Contents

Preface

When I was in my twenties, like most people I used to think that middle age was not something to look forward to. I think it was Dante in *The Divine Comedy* who described midlife as being akin to finding yourself in the middle of a dark forest, and that about summed it up. It seemed like a deadening period of life in which you just coasted along, getting greyer every day both physically and mentally. Men and women seemed to peak in their thirties and then just seemed to slide into becoming all the things that I didn't like about people: authoritarian, overweight, over-opinionated, safe and very, very conventional.

I was wrong. Dante wasn't stating a fact about midlife, he was just lost. It doesn't have to be like that at all, as I hope you will agree when you've read this book. In compiling it I have tried to give you, the reader, up-to-date information and opinions about midlife so that you will be able to get a better perspective of what actually happens and what you can do about the changes that occur. What I've tried above all to do is to show you how poorly we have understood midlife and its challenges. It is in fact an exciting and enormously important stage of life which has become increasingly so as people live longer and healthier lives.

But the book is a very practical study. Colleagues, patients and friends going through midlife often raised points, questions or issues I had no answer to, and it was out of this need that I thought about writing a book that dealt broadly with the period, not just, say, with the menopause or ageing.

There was also a more personal motive for tackling midlife issues. As I approached midlife I wasn't a pretty sight. I was overweight, over-worked, under-exercised and not very happy. I was becoming the very thing that I had not wanted to become – a grey unhealthy midlifer. Just another statistic. For a whole range of reasons I changed: not all of them, I must confess, due to an act of will on my part. I'm now 48, almost as fit and healthy as I was in my twenties and about six times happier. It wasn't a picnic, but once I'd begun the process of change it became easier to build on the gains until I could feel more in control of my life and my development as an individual.

So, in writing this book I did so from two perspectives: first as a clinician and secondly as someone who is actively engaged in the process of being middle-aged and who is still working at it. If I can do it – so can you.

Introduction

There was a time, not so long ago, when the word 'middle-aged' had a depressing connotation. It conjured up an image of grey-haired, suburban blandness; no excitement, no style, no sex. For many people, particularly young people, old age started once you had reached the age of 40; goodbye youth, fun and games, hello menopause, old age and, somewhere lurking in the background, death. Popular opinion used to have it that midlife signalled the beginning of the end of life as we know it and the onset of midlife was bad news – no matter how many books you read promising you that life really did begin at 40. All the really interesting events in life took place in the first 40 years; thereafter you could expect little more than ill health, declining fitness and, if you were unlucky, a long slide into senility. When you entered middle age you automatically became a member of a marginal group with your own clubs, your own magazines and television programmes – even your own package tours. All were designed to help you face the Big Challenges ahead; baldness, grey hair, wrinkles and how to cope with retirement.

It was worse if you were a woman. There was the dreaded menopause to worry about, the time that your periods stopped, your hormones did strange things and had strange effects. Some women went through untold misery adjusting to the change. Would this happen to you? Would you need tranquillizers, hormone treatment or perhaps a hysterectomy? Or would you be one of the few lucky ones to slip through unscathed without having to spend your days watching your medication?

There was also the risk that you might turn out to be one of those unhappy people who experience a midlife crisis and who never seem to be the same again. Once more, so popular opinion had it, this tended to be worse if you were a woman because women seemed more likely to suffer mental collapse than men during their crises. Women who rebelled in midlife were more often deemed to be in need of psychiatric help than men, and often ended up permanently neurotic or depressed. In contrast, men who broke down in midlife seemed to end up running off with nubile young women or blowing the family fortunes on bright red sports cars or crates of champagne. Literature and history is full of examples (mainly male) of apparently perfectly ordinary people who out of the blue go off the rails; people like Gauguin – once a stockbroker – who ran off to the South Pacific, or Simenon's character, Monsieur Monde, who decided one day to take a different train and abandoned his job, his wife and family.

These however were the exceptions to the rule. Most people, it was supposed, settled into midlife after a youth spent rebelling and sowing their wild oats. People were expected to have matured by then and be ready to slow down and take their place in conventional society; middle-aged people were inevitably in the majority on school boards, they were often justices of the peace, respected doctors, successful businessmen, stalwarts of industry, the community and the family – the people who laid down the law, the people who you turned to for advice and wisdom. More than any other age group they were seen as the representatives of society, the upholders of its values. They were the people that younger folk rebelled against.

Midlife it was believed was grey, yes, and boring, but it was supposedly a settled, comfortable, mature time. If you didn't fit in, if you rebelled, you were considered strange, eccentric perhaps, but above all immature. Think of the ways in which such rebels were described: 'She's running away from her responsibilities'; or 'He's just having a second childhood'.

This was how we used to think about midlife and is probably how many people still think about it. Yet those of us who are midlifers or who work with or study them have a very different picture. Things seem to have changed radically over the last decade.

In the past, for example, little attention was paid to middle-aged people. The media were never interested in them as a social group and they were seldom in the public eye. These days though they are prominent in ways they never were in bygone eras; the adventures of Richard Branson, Chris Bonnington, or Ranulph Fiennes make headlines despite the fact that they are no longer in the prime of their youth. In the performing arts midlifers like the Rolling Stones, George Harrison, Bob Dylan, Peter O'Toole, Tina Turner, Paul Hogan, Clint Eastwood, Oliver Stone, Cher and Eric Clapton command enormous attention. And much of the music of today reflects the preferences and influences of middle-aged people: The Doors, Roy Orbison, Paul Simon, Paul McCartney. . .

Midlifers today are also refusing to grow old gracefully; never have middle-aged people been so concerned about how they look and how they dress. They fill the gyms trying to stay fit; they watch what they eat; they're almost obsessively interested in health and fitness.

At a different level, thousands of perfectly ordinary middle-aged people are exploring new ways of thinking; they are interested in all sorts of growth movements such as yoga, T'ai Chi, alternative medicine, spiritualism, religion and psychotherapy. They are curious about themselves and are seeking a deeper understanding of life, the universe and their place in it. More importantly though these interests are essentially unorthodox, rebellious even; they fall outside the range of prescribed middle-aged interests. In the past, middle-aged people tended to remain strictly within the range of orthodox social thinking and belief. Today, your average middle-aged bank manager may look just like his counterpart of a generation ago (it was virtually impossible to find a woman bank manager then) but there is now a strong possibility that out of working hours she or he may be a practising Buddhist, drive a Honda Gold Wing or be planning a holiday exploring little-known Himalayan hill trails.

These interests are more than just philosophical. They reflect the intense questioning of the *status quo* – the way middle-aged life is meant to be – that midlifers everywhere are engaging in. This search for meaning is an indicator of the deep dissatisfaction midlifers have for the orthodox interpretation of midlife. That this questioning is more than a spiritual quest or an intellectual exercise can be seen in the way that they are *acting* on their feelings and ideas. They are changing the way they live and how they relate: the structure of relationships between men and women is changing and, with it, notions about marital and family life. Significantly, divorce rates are higher now than they have ever been and there are more single-parent families than at any other time this century.

Relationships have been slowly changing since the 1960s and many of the people involved in these changes today are middle-aged. Many are women rebelling against the roles that they have been forced for years to accept in marriage and the family. Midlife women are tired of being 'only' wives and mothers – they want the freedom to make a mark on the world, to do something with their lives in addition to being a partner in a relationship or the mother of children. Some middle-aged men are similarly frustrated with their roles as breadwinners, of trying to live up to the popular images of maleness that they have been brought up with. They want a break from trying to achieve, from having to be decisive, calm, thoughtful, responsible and unemotional. They want to explore, without feeling guilty, aspects of their personalities that they have previously learned to repress or hide away.

Many midlife people are struggling with these dilemmas; they feel dissatisfied with their lives. While they may have jobs and be comfortably off, many aren't sure they are doing what they want. There is a strong movement, for example, to get back to basics, to get away from the sophisticated life-styles of modern cities, back to nature, back to more fulfilling jobs and relationships. They feel constrained by their relationships, unfulfilled in their marriages; they feel distanced from their own children and from their own parents and have trouble relating to both. They feel sometimes like a lost generation, not fitting in with the values and ideas of either the younger generation or the older. Many midlifers today were active participators in the social movements of the radical 1960s and feel they have lost their way – after sex'n'drugs and rock'n'roll *and* straight living they still haven't found what they are looking for.

For both men and women it's important to realize that midlife can present the opportunity to act on these feelings. Job security and financial considerations are often easier when you're middle-aged than when you were younger, and your children may have left home or will shortly do so, giving you the time and space to reflect. The immediate pressure of obligation and guilt lifts somewhat. There is time to think, time to act, time to change.

Many contemporary 40- and 50-year-olds have understood this and seem to be quietly challenging all the old adages about settling down into a peaceful and conformist middle age. There has been a revolution in style. In many ways midlifers have

become rebellious. Not the radical, explosive rebellion of adolescence and early adulthood, but a quieter, more thorough
questioning of the *status quo*. Moreover, this feeling is not
limited to a handful of eccentric misfits but seems to be a
widespread phenomenon. Midlife rebellion seems to be assu-
ming the proportions of a social movement, irrespective of
income, class and social position.

Why is this? Why is it that today we are seeing so many
midlifers openly challenging the conventions of society? What
is it all about?

There are many reasons why this is happening now, which
we will explore in this book, but in a fundamental sense what
we are seeing has to do with a change in individual awareness.
People now entering the midlife period have benefited from
the stability provided by nearly half a century of peace, economic prosperity and social continuity since the end of the
Second World War. Men and women in their forties and fifties
today are better-off, healthier, better educated and can expect
to live longer than at any other time in history. One of the
consequences of this is that more people than ever now have
the time, energy and intellectual freedom to reflect on what
they are doing and where they are going. In previous epochs
economic hardships, wars, ill-health and the psychological
constraints imposed by duty and religion left little time to rebel
against the accepted wisdom of the day. You rebelled and sowed
your wild oats when you were young and spent the rest of your
life paying for it. Life was short and old age started early.

Midlifers today seem to have turned this around. Whereas
in the past it was the educated or wealthy few who might have
had the time and money to reflect on society and its dictates,
most midlifers now concern themselves with these issues.
They are much more inclined to reflect on what and who they
are than their parents and grandparents were.

Rebellions, however, are not easy things to manage at any
age. Challenging the *status quo* is always a risky thing no matter
who you are. It raises a lot of questions and can cause a great
deal of guilt, uncertainty and anxiety, especially if you feel you
are supposed to be past all that – mature, grown up, a pillar
of society. You wonder if you're right to feel dissatisfied with
your lot in life. You wonder why you are no longer satisfied
with roles that you were happy to play for years. You wonder
if there is something wrong with you.

This is where this book comes in. Many midlifers need to know more about the kinds of emotional, psychological and relational challenges they and others of their generation face. They need to know why so many midlifers are dissatisfied and want to do something about it.

Unfulfilled dreams play a large part in this dissatisfaction. An important process of rebelling is the struggle to realize day-dreams or dream-maps. As young children we begin constructing dream-maps of our ideal world and continue to build on them throughout our lives. Working towards such dreams or fantasies is an integral part of individuation; it is when we lose sight of our dream-maps, or come nowhere near fulfilling them, that we run into difficulties. Midlife offers the opportunity to re-examine our lives in relation to our dream-maps.

Now it's time to fulfil your personal responsibility to yourself as *an individual*, to look again at that secret dreaming part of yourself and give it the opportunity to develop and grow.

All too often, however, when midlifers seek help about their feelings and aspirations, they are offered opinions that are frequently out of date, with little relevance for today's midlifer. The vast majority of lay and professional people still see the midlife period and its crises as being dominated by organic changes or physiological crises – the result of ageing, intellectual deterioration or physiological changes in the body that can cause distress or discomfort unless properly confronted. This assumption is reflected in books and magazine articles dealing with midlife. Practically all focus on its somatic, or physiological aspects and offer health and dietary advice. Practically all the popular medical books on the subject deal exclusively with organic (mainly hormonal) approaches to midlife problems, and the remedies offered – ranging from tranquillizers to hormone replacement therapy – inevitably involve medical procedures or psychiatric treatment of one kind or another.

While undoubtedly some people do experience disturbing somatic changes during the midlife period, there has in general been a neglect by professionals and the public of major inter-personal and psychological challenges that occur during the midlife period. Fortunately there is a growing appreciation amongst some professionals that midlife is much more complex than was previously thought. The midlife period has always been seen as a marginal, transitory phase – a period in which you simply marked time between the excitement of young adulthood and the decline of old age. Now however there is mounting evidence that intelligence and other abilities and drives do not necessarily deteriorate with age and in fact can become enhanced, can broaden and deepen. It is slowly becoming recognized that the physiological element is only one element in a very much more complex set of challenges that are presented in midlife.

This book presents a completely fresh way of looking at midlife, incorporating this new thinking about the challenges involved over this period. Midlife is perhaps the most important of all life's stages precisely because it presents an opportunity for people to re-examine the way they have lived in the past. Life is full of problems to solve and stresses to face and people learn as young adults to cope in socially acceptable ways without disrupting the established order of things. Most of us knuckle down and cope, too busy managing our jobs, looking after our children or paying the mortgage to question what we are doing. It is often only during the midlife period that there is opportunity to reflect on how we have managed in the past.

In a fundamental sense many of today's midlifers are far ahead of professional understanding of middle age. Some are already leading lives of rebellion and personal evolution, meeting challenges head on, with or without the support of their families or their societies. These acts of rebellion may result in antagonism, conflict or bewilderment from those close to the person – their partners, families, work colleagues. Sometimes, faced with these feelings and the resulting anxiety and guilt, midlifers may become depressed or nervous, or may rebel too recklessly to preserve the momentum of the changes they want to make.

This book is about improving the quality of life and the quality of relationships. These concerns are after all what most midlife rebellions are about. The central focus of this book is on relationships, and with good reason. Relationships dominate our lives and they do so in ways that most people are unaware of. They help to shape our personalities. As we grow up, the relationship we have with our parents can dictate how we work, how we relate to other people, what kind of lives we lead. Our marital relationships and our relationships with our own children can fulfil our emotional needs beyond our wildest dreams, but they can also be a source of distress and despair.

These relationships can give us strength and security but they can also cripple us.

The relationships we have can also affect our health. Heart disease and cancer, for example, have been linked to a range of personality styles, some of which we may have been taught as children. Relationships can help make people vulnerable to some diseases and they can also help us to recover from accidents and illnesses.

Little wonder then that all sorts of problems and crises can occur when relationships change or come apart as they so often do in midlife. The book aims to help people make sense of the psychological, emotional and physical events that they or their partners are experiencing. We will not treat midlife and its crises as a simple matter of biological deterioration or the search for an elixir of youth through the use of medication, diet or spiritual philosophies. The emphasis in the book is on how to recognize your stresses and dissatisfactions, how to cope with them and how to rebel in a constructive and healthy way.

We'll be looking too at how some midlifers have managed to achieve their goals as well as how and why some others have failed. So if you're over 35 and beginning to think about what midlife crises you may be heading for, or if you're well into midlife and want to sort yourself out, you should be able to get some idea of what's involved from what follows in this book.

For my mother, Irene, with love

Acknowledgements

I would like to thank the following people for the help they have given me in the preparation of this book:
Peter Athanasiou, Louis Baum, Merle Baum, Teresa Brennan, Brigitte Herant-Dunais, Saskia Handley, Brenda Hart, Jane Kondou, Andreas Koskinas, Catherine Lambley, Carol McCoulough, Julia McCutchen, Shelley Power, Gerassimos Rigatos, Penny Sandler and Wolfgang Pick.

Naturally, all ideas expressed except where otherwise stated are my responsibility.

CHAPTER ONE

A Fresh Look at Midlife and its Crises

Compared to the physical changes, the trials and tribulations of childhood and adolescence, and the uncomfortable decline of old age, adulthood seems a relatively calm period, at least biologically. If you assume the average life-span of a human is approximately 70 years and the first 20 years involve growth and the last 10 decline, the period of adulthood affords the longest stretch of about 40 years of relatively untroubled biological functioning. Except, that is, for one potential blot on the landscape – the midlife period.

Most people, especially young people and those yet to reach midlife, regard it as a period of emotional turmoil. There are significant biological implications linked to the fact that the menopause in women occurs during the same period. Most of the images used to describe middle age are essentially negative ones, usually involving various permutations of the concept of ageing. In fact, in our youth-orientated society, being middle-aged means being old, and being elderly – that is, over 60 – means being *really* old.

So what exactly is midlife? To get an idea of what it is that we are talking about let's look first at how the midlife period has been seen historically in our own society and go on from there.

A LITTLE HISTORY

Throughout the Western historical tradition and up until relatively recently, midlife was not regarded as an especially

1

Some technical terms

The word generally used to refer to the midlife period whether for male or female is the *climacteric*. This comes from the Ancient Greek work *klimakterikos* which was originally an astrological term used to signify critical periods in human life based on cycles of seven or nine years. You find this notion in Hippocrates' system for describing the seven ages of life, in which each climacteric is marked by a critical task or tasks. The *menopause* refers to the cessation of the monthly periods in women: *mén* means 'month' in Greek, hence *emmenopausis* 'monthly pause'.

---

difficult period. There has always been an association between the biological changes of midlife and the waning of biological drives usually defined in sexual or reproductive terms. It has always been observed, for example, that some men may experience a reduction in their sexual drive during the midlife period when, as one author quaintly put it, 'the male genital system begins to wane'. Similarly, there has always been a limit to how long women can produce children.

Most early writings, where they mention midlife or the menopause at all, talk about finding ways of restoring the vigour of youth, especially in men. We are all familiar with the historical search for the elixir of youth, and this was usually the concern of the middle-aged and wealthy. By and large, though, these practices were seen as a normal part of the ageing process and it was considered quite natural that people should try to put the biological clock back if they had the time and money to make the effort.

The female climacteric

The midlife climacteric in women has always been regarded differently from that of men. This is not surprising since women have also traditionally been thought to have a different psychology as well as physiology from men based on the fact

Remedies for midlife

One of the earliest recorded remedies for midlife impotence was extract of donkey penis as recommended by Ancient Egyptian doctors. Not that we've come much further in recent centuries: a 19th century French doctor reportedly cured his and his wife's problems using canine testicular juice, and let us not forget the enormous ongoing world-wide trade in exotic aphrodisiacs such as crushed rhino horn. For a long time there was little else to try apart from the traditional folkloristic remedies and over the years all sorts of glandular extracts were used without success. The discovery of the natural oestrogens in the 1920s was the first real step in the right direction, but it wasn't until after 1960 that effective hormonal preparations became widely available.

that they have a womb and men don't. The womb has had a mixed reception in history and has often been blamed for quite a large part of what men don't understand about the behaviour of women. On the one hand it has been seen as useful in that it permits women to have children and so continue the human race. But it has also been held responsible for a wide range of female emotional problems: the term 'hysteria' derives from the Greek word for 'womb'. In ancient times, the womb was regarded by Hippocrates as holding an almost supernatural power over a woman for much of her life until it 'died' during the midlife climacteric. This idea has persisted down through the ages and accounts in part for why the onset of the menopause has often been considered something of a mixed blessing; a sign that at last a woman could face life free from the awesome power of the womb and its attendant emotions and, at the same time, evidence that her period of fertility is over.

We should not be too surprised that midlife and its problems are rarely mentioned in Western history. There were rather more pressing issues to contend with for the average citizen. People spent a lot less time on earth than they do now and what little time they had to live was usually taken up with surviving wars, famine, disease and other troubles. Most people

people didn't expect to live much longer than the midlife climacteric anyway, and you were considered old by the time you reached 40.

What helped to change this relative lack of formal interest in midlife was the gradual rise in the status and power of medicine which coincided with the rise of the industrialized societies of Europe and America. Doctors began to write books, and it is from these early records that we can see mention being made of midlife problems, almost all of them concentrating on the problems experienced by women.

The female menopause

In the 18th century there were scattered references to the more familiar signs and symptoms we associate with the menopause today. John Leake, an English physician, noted in 1777 in one of the earliest published medical textbooks that women during midlife sometimes experienced headaches, dizziness, colic pains and a range of 'female' hysteric disorders. Leake was also one of the first to write about the association between the appearance of chronic diseases and the loss of periods in women and this helped to establish the notion that physical as well as emotional problems occurred at about the same time. But it wasn't until the 19th century that doctors in general really began to believe that there was something more than hysteria going on during the midlife of women.

Most doctors in Britain and America subscribed to the traditional view that little of medical interest happened during the menopause, but in France as early as 1816, reports appeared describing a 'menopausal' syndrome that required treatment. By mid-century, British and American doctors followed suit and the medicalization of the midlife period began.

This association of organic pathology and emotional problems with the menopause slowly gained favour in medical circles as the 19th century progressed. Two medical approaches to midlife emerged, the gynaecological and psychiatric, comprising the two kinds of doctors who had most to do with midlife women and the problems of which they complained. Gynaecologists seeking to understand the workings of the womb soon focused on the role played by the ovaries and

---

Signs and symptoms

The list of problems associated with the midlife climacteric is vast. Biological signs include hot flushes, dizziness, palpitations, headaches, diarrhoea, constipation, cramps, vaginal and skin dryness and general body discomfort in women; loss of potency and erectile failure in men. Psychological symptoms include depression, lethargy, hysteria, insomnia, nervousness, irritability, distress, loss of concentration, confidence and, sometimes, sexual desire.

A 19th-century view

Dr Edward Tilt, a fashionable ladies' doctor who had travelled in France, was amongst the first in Britain to go against the then prevailing opinion when he opened a practice in London in the 1850s. Tilt listed nervous irritability, hysterical states and unrealistic melancholia as being common during the female midlife period. However, he tended to treat the condition cautiously (advising his patients to take health cures at resorts and where possible to avoid over-stimulating the sexual organs) and retained the ancient view of the power of the womb, attributing most of the symptoms he treated to pathologies in the womb, including the increased sexual drive he sometimes observed in his middle-aged female patients.

---

hormones in the female reproductive cycle, and came up with the idea that problems encountered by women in midlife were due to changes in these.

Psychiatry, on the other hand, arose almost entirely out of the need for doctors to take care of the insane, and it's worth bearing this in mind because it seems to have played no small part in the theories that they developed about midlife. Initially, as you can imagine, psychiatrists became interested in midlife problems because there was the suggestion that emotional difficulties were often noted in menopausal women. As they turned their attention to the subject, a possible link to the more extreme forms of mental instability became increasingly commented upon.

By far the biggest boost to this way of thinking about the menopause came from the eminent German psychiatrist, Emil Kraepelin, one of the founders of scientific psychiatry. Kraepelin introduced the notion of 'involutional psychosis' in 1906, arguing that this serious form of psychosis seemed to occur mainly in women during their menopausal years and it was characterized by agitation, hypochondriasis and sets of delusions related to intense guilt and anxiety.

At about the same time that psychiatry was flexing its muscles, two other closely related disciplines were beginning to study the human psyche and were to have a major impact on public opinion. Psychology and psychoanalysis rose to prominence in the early part of the 20th century, and unlike the psychiatric tradition which focused on managing disturbed people in mental hospitals, these two disciplines studied or treated a range of relatively normal problems. Just as gynaecologists tended to reduce the wealth of midlife experience to the theories they developed to explain the problems of their patients, so psychologists and psychoanalysts tended to see apparently normal growing events in terms of the complex, often pathology-driven theories they derived from their patients.

Not unexpectedly, some influential psychoanalytic writers saw the midlife period as a major symbolic life-event with, by and large, negative connotations. Helen Deutsch, for example, saw the menopause as a time of great loss of femininity derived from the loss of the ability to reproduce. It is also from the psychoanalytic literature that we get the suggestion that reaction to midlife changes in women and men can lead to regression and childlike thoughts and behaviours.

In some ways the influence of psychoanalysis on public opinion has been even more thorough than the ideas derived from gynaecology and psychiatry. Part of this was due to the fact that psychoanalytic thought influenced far more people and reached more strata of society than those of the other professions. Psychoanalysis influenced a whole range of non-medical people like writers, artists and film makers. Ultimately these ideas strengthened the view that midlife was a time of trouble, be it physiological or psychological.

Over the top?

It wasn't until the 1960s that effective hormone-boosting medications became available, but once they were, they helped to strengthen gynaecological interpretations of the menopause. One school of gynaecological thought regarded the menopause as a midlife disease. Thus one gynaecologist wrote in 1963: 'The menopausal woman is not normal; she suffers from a deficiency disease with serious sequelae and needs treatment'. Similarly, when psychoanalysis was at the peak of its popularity, one writer suggested that women can regress during menopause to infantile obsessions with, amongst other things, penis envy. (Could this explain the hot flush!)

The male menopause

Most of the ideas on female midlife crises have arisen out of what we could regard as an over-emphasis on the menopause in women, but men haven't fared much better. Although the male climacteric is supposed to occur somewhat later than that of women, male midlife crises have also been reduced to biological or emotional deficiencies. Some doctors, for example, argue that men who experience a waning of their sexual powers during midlife are suffering from the male hormone deficiencies and are therefore in need of treatment. Similarly, men who go off the rails and complain of emotional difficulties or sexual boredom are thought by some schools of psychiatry to be suffering from mental problems that require psychoanalysis or other forms of therapy to put right.

The odd thing, though, is that while it is women who are thought to become depressed and show a range of psychological reactions including hysteria, irritability, depression and neurosis during midlife, it is men who are reported to go really off the rails at the climacteric moment. It is men who go the whole hog and change their lives radically. We've already talked about Gauguin, who in midlife abandoned career and family in search of the elixir of life. But Leo Tolstoy, the Russian writer, underwent a midlife crisis during which he turned religious and rejected his earlier writings. And we all know of staid middle-aged men who suddenly go off with younger women, apparently to stave off the effects of ageing and the loss of energy and vigour.

MIDLIFE AS DISORDER

You can see from this brief look at the history of our thinking about midlife that by and large it has been characterized as a time of distress and difficulty, and that signs of rebellion and other crises in men or women have been taken as indicators of disorder. The midlife rebel, the person who has problems, according to this tradition has either a biological deficiency or an emotional deficiency, both of which need treatment. In fact if you're a woman you're probably familiar with how this works. If you're having problems with your menopause and you visit a gynaecologist, the chances are that you'll be told you have a biological disorder 'associated with menopause' and you'll be treated accordingly. If instead you visit a psychiatrist, the chances are you'll be told you have an emotional or psychiatric disorder 'associated with the menopause' and, again, be treated accordingly.

Is this all there is to midlife? Is it as negative as it is painted? Are midlife crises simply the results of hormones gone wrong or drying up? Can hormonal changes alone have such a (sometimes) devastating effect? Are midlife rebels really only just immature people who have never grown up? There are other schools of thought, other traditions of research, that paint a very different and much fuller picture of midlife. They are not however so well known, nor have they had the same kind of influence on popular thinking.

Other cultures

Anthropological and cross-cultural research has taught us that this popular view of midlife and its crises is not necessarily universally experienced. While ageing is a universal phenomenon, how the signs of ageing are treated varies from culture to culture and even within the same culture. In many pre-technological communities, for example, ageing brings with it in-

Funny you should say that

I can remember a professor of psychiatry, a conservative man of the old school, painting a lurid picture of men in midlife who suffered emotional crises. You could always tell, he said, when they had entered the critical phase; they tended to go for bright colours and flashy actions when previously they had been ultra-conservative, even dowdy. He proved this point rather interestingly when a year later, shortly after his fiftieth birthday, I saw him climb into his new bright red Alfa Romeo wearing a bright yellow polo-neck sweater and a white suit chatting ardently to the rather attractive young blonde who was with him.

creased status and respect. Elder people are often regarded as the bearers and teachers of wisdom: amongst hunter tribes it is often the older men who lead and guide the hunt, blending the youthful prowess and speed of the younger men with their own wisdom and knowledge. In these isolated societies, free of the large-scale changes and pressures that characterize more technologically advanced cultures, there is a transition from youth to old age with few of the problems we associate with midlife.

Even amongst technologically advanced societies the meaning and symptoms of midlife vary quite markedly. Japan offers a fascinating example of how important a part cultural and social valuations play in the meaning we give to midlife. This modern industrial nation is comparable to the advanced industrial nations of the West, with similar economic values and similar standards of living. Yet traditionally, midlife, especially amongst women, has not had the same meaning as in Western industrialized societies. Japanese society continues to regard the midlife period as marking the onset of maturity rather than just the onset of old age – until they have reached the age of 50, most Japanese people are not considered fully mature.

Although the cessation of periods in Japanese women is seen as part of the change of life, it is not given the central role it assumes amongst Western women. Even the symptoms are different. Hot flushes – the single most frequently reported

---

It depends on your point of view

In some cultures, where the ageing signs that so pre-occupy us are hard to see, cessation of a woman's repro-ductive capability is the only visible sign of the onset of midlife, but how this is reacted to varies considerably. Some studies of African women show that it is taken as a positive sign indicating an improvement in social status following the removal of menstrual taboos. In other tribes, though, it can mean a loss of status since the woman can no longer bear children. The Rajput women of northern India report few menopausal symptoms, largely, it is believed, because after the menopause they may emerge from purdah and move freely around their villages for the first time since youth.

---

complaint amongst Western women – are uncommon amongst Japanese women. While they report some complaints in com-mon with Western women during the menopause, notably constipation and diarrhoea, the most common complaint is a stiffness in the shoulder. The next most common is headaches.

In recent years the notion of a menopausal syndrome has however begun to appear in Japanese medical circles where it is considered a new form of illness, as a kind of luxury disease affecting women with too much time on their hands who run to doctors with their insignificant complaints'. Some authors have noted that this has coincided with government efforts to cope with an increasingly ageing population by encouraging middle-aged women to stay at home and look after the elderly, thereby sparing the state the task. Margaret Locke, a medical anthropologist, suggests that many middle-aged women resent this restriction on their new-found midlife freedom and have reacted in the only way they know how – by complaining of physical difficulties. As she says, 'Menopause thus acts as a lightning-rod for contested social issues.'

Attitudes to midlife are by no means uniform, even amongst Western societies. In one cross-national study in Europe, for example, overall more than half the women questioned had found the menopause psychologically upsetting, but while two thirds of French and British women had found it distressing, this was not the case with German women, amongst whom fewer than half had found it difficult psychologically. Even within these societies, patterns vary. Women whose periods started late, those who never married, those who had never fallen pregnant and those who had a child after the age of 40 seemed to be less affected by the menopause than other women. Wealth and education also seem to help, with better-off and better-educated women tending to report fewer problems with the menopause.

You can see from this that while we may all think we have a pretty clear idea about what midlife and its crises involve, far too much of what we think we know is specific to our own society and far too much has been coloured by what we think we know about the menopause. When you mention the word 'midlife', most people automatically jump to the conclusion that you're talking about the menopause (in men and women). We don't even have a word for the male midlife climacteric. What I've tried to show so far is that the picture is not quite so simple. A number of events take place during the midlife period – we undergo biological changes, for example – but how we react to them seems to be determined by the circumstances in which we live. More importantly, it seems that what happens during midlife can't simply be reduced to the physical changes that we automatically assume are the cause of midlife problems. Much more is involved; many other events also come together during the same period and in concentrating on the menopause we have lost track of how important it is to think about what else happens at the same time.

Where do our ideas about midlife come from?

What I want to suggest is that we have, in a sense, been brainwashed about midlife. Perhaps brainwashed is a strong word, but let me at least say that our ideas about midlife have arisen unquestioned out of contemporary folklore; a folklore that has been based on only part – the medical interpretation – of the overall picture.

Think for a moment where your ideas about midlife have come from. Imagine if you like that you have no personal experience of midlife but it's drawing closer and you begin for the first time to wonder about it. Part of the picture you have built up will have been gathered from personal contact with people who have been through midlife or are currently experiencing it. Some of it will be second- or third-hand information; stories about relatives who had a difficult time or someone you vaguely know doing something strange that was labelled irresponsible or part of the menopause. Nine times out of ten what you will hear will be bad news; you're less likely to hear about people who had a good midlife period or who hardly noticed the menopause than those who had a difficult time, who did strange things or needed help in one form or another. Some of your information will have been gleaned from the media, from books, magazines, documentaries or films you have read or seen: Edward Albee's *Who's afraid of Virginia Woolf?* didn't exactly paint a glowing picture of a couple at midlife. Again, most of what you see or read homes in on the difficult parts of midlife and especially on the physical difficulties. It is only when you stand back and look at the whole picture that you can get an accurate idea of what is really going on.

Even doctors only see part of the story, and quite naturally so, since they are often only consulted when there are physical problems to be dealt with. Little wonder then that they focus so much on the somatic manifestations of midlife and think about it in terms of what medical, pharmacological or surgical help can be given.

This is an important point. We place a great deal of faith in medical views often without realizing that medical science can have limitations. Medicine is also full of controversy. Many of the early ideas about midlife have been challenged within medicine itself, but we hear little about this in the media. Many of the cherished beliefs about menopause passed down from generation to generation of doctors were based on very poor research and sampling procedures, and this has been pointed out by a number of researchers. Some of the 19th-century ideas, for example, were based on samples of female mental patients, thus confusing midlife with a whole range of other factors.

There are many gynaecologists too who do not agree with the current direction taken with the treatment of menopausal difficulties. And most psychiatric researchers today believe that

Way to go, Harry

The way studies are reported can sometimes be misleading. For example, there was a recent study about the sexual experience of American men widely reported in the media which showed that the average lifetime number of sexual partners for men in the study was about 16. Careful reading of the results however showed that the most frequently occurring response was only seven. The higher average result occurred because a handful of men reported huge numbers of sexual partners and this raised the average. Those people who didn't know the difference between an average and the frequency measure would jump to the conclusion that most men have 16 partners, which was the case with Harry, one of my more unconfident middle-aged patients, who rushed in with a copy of the report, demanding to know what was wrong with him for having slept with so few women. It took a while to sort this out.

far more is involved during midlife than the biological changes that we are familiar with. These alternative views have not been widely reported in the media, neither have they had much effect on popular views about the menopause.

Much of the scientific data presented as evidence for theories needs to be very carefully examined. Scientific research is perhaps the most potent means we have of gaining knowledge, but it is an immensely intricate process that takes place in a very complex context. The scientific community, the context in which research is conducted and evaluated, is continually checking and testing theories and evaluating research to the extent that, in any given field, there are very few finally settled issues, and there can be as many explanations for research studies as there are scientists working in the field. The difficulty comes when scientific studies are taken (or reported) out of this context. When this happens, the results of a study are interpreted in isolation and without the reader being aware of all the other issues involved and of conflicting studies that may have been conducted.

Sorry, folks, we were wrong

When I was training 25 years ago, we were taught that women were prone to develop involutional melancholia (or involutional psychosis) during midlife. As we saw earlier, this unpleasant mental illness was first introduced by Kraepelin. What we were not taught was that Kraepelin subsequently changed his mind about the existence of the condition, and that many other psychiatrists and gynaecologists had long since stopped associating the condition with the menopause in women. But such is the power of suggestion and tradition that the idea persisted precisely because it fitted into the general psychiatric and clinical folklore of the time. It wasn't in fact until 1979 that this form of psychosis was finally dropped from the guidance manual produced by the American Psychiatric Association. Like homosexuality, which also used to be considered a mental disorder and was eventually dropped from manuals, involutional psychosis no longer theoretically exists.

Similarly, Dr Barbara Ballinger, in an extensive review of the field published in 1990, pointed out that general population studies (studies conducted on a broad range of women rather than on a narrow range of troubled women) showed that the menopause did not cause unusual mental problems for women. She noted that social, cultural and family pressures are now thought to be more relevant to problems that menopausal women report. If anything, she suggested, mental problems were more prevalent amongst women in the five years before menopause, that is, well before the onset of physiological changes.

A BROADER VIEW

So where do we go from here? Let me try to re-define the notion of midlife in a way that reflects the broader research and thinking that we have looked at so far. A good way to think about midlife is to see it as a series of overlays.

The biological overlay

One of the best ways to understand midlife is to start with the notion of the life-cycle. We are, after all, living organisms and we have biological patterns that are dictated by our physiological constitution. Most of the activity of our body is organized into rhythmic cycles – rest/activity cycles, sleep/wake cycles, monthly cycles and so on. This is, if you like, the Procrustean overlay, one of several sets of overlays that define our lives. Birth, growth, decline and death are part of the biological overlay we share with other animals. The midlife climacteric fits in somewhere between growth and decline and is a convenient way we use to talk about one of the epochs of the life-cycle just as we talk about childhood or adolescence. We should not forget that the words we use to describe them are shorthand ways of referring to complex periods; we should not use them in an absolute biological sense. Decline, like growth, is a long, subtle and gradual process; the biological periods we associate with childhood, adolescence and midlife can take ten or fifteen years from beginning to end, if not longer, and very much more than biology is involved. Biological changes take place during midlife but they are by no means absolute and other overlays also play a part in what happens.

The social overlay

The second overlay is provided by the social or cultural environment in which we live. Societies or communities are found in the animal as well as human world and they share the same function: to organize interaction, to systematize ways of behaving so that the members of a community can co-exist, share geographical space and resources, and fulfil their biological drives. Societies and cultures create mores for life and its cycles in order to facilitate organization and communication; mores are sets of beliefs about what is happening and what to do. Thus societies have prescriptions for every major stage and event in life; we have beliefs and expectations about childhood behaviour, about adolescence, about how people should live together and so on. Society generates these beliefs as sets of shared ideas and they are transmitted through the family, teachers and the media to members growing up in the community. They are so thoroughly transmitted in fact that most of us grow up believing in them completely without realizing that they are not necessarily absolute and that some of our most cherished beliefs and ways of doing things are not necessarily shared by other communities.

Many factors help to determine the social interpretations and explanatory mores used in any given society. Economic and political circumstances, moral and religious beliefs, for example, all help to give shape and direction to social beliefs about the midlife period. We saw from the Japanese data how social beliefs can be shaped in part by economic and political factors, like the need to keep middle-aged women at home to help look after the family and save the state expense on social facilities. We can also see that technologically advanced societies with their pharmaceutical industries and medical infrastructures tend to approach midlife and its problems in ways that fit conveniently into these existing frameworks. The system thus tends to favour ideas it is geared to cope with rather than ideas which may require change and cost time and money.

In addition, we should note that how societies view and use women helps also to shape the midlife mores used in any given society. If a society needed middle-aged women to do more than sit at home and look after the elderly, you can be sure the problems of midlife would be minimized. Think of what happened to the role of women during the two world wars. Similarly, society helps to create the mores we have in family life. The Western family has changed over the 20th century; we have smaller families now and we encourage our children to be more independent once they are old enough to leave home. One result is that when children leave home they often move away at about the midlife period of their parents, thus creating a specific effect that might be absent in communities with a stronger tradition of families staying closer together.

You can see that when midlife comes along, not only has our society helped to shape what happens, but it has ensured that we are ready with a set of beliefs and expectations which we use to account for whatever changes materialize.

The personal overlay

We are all exposed to similar biological and social challenges as we grow up but we each form our own set ways of coping

The Tolstoys

A good example of the way that society helps to shape how we think about midlife is provided by the different perspectives we have on the midlife crises of the Russian author, Tolstoy, and his wife, Sofia. Tolstoy is supposed to have experienced increasingly severe episodes of emotional distress from the age of 45 onwards while working on *Anna Karenina*. These culminated in a type of existential crisis over the meaning of life and a religious conversion at the age of 50. He made an abrupt break with his own literary past as a consequence, and devoted the remainder of his life to propagating his religious ideas. His midlife crisis, if we can call it that, has often been interpreted as arising over anxiety about facing death and seems to have intensified with his ageing and his gradual realization that there was a physical limit to what he could achieve in his own lifetime.

Tolstoy was by most accounts always a difficult and emotionally and sexually troubled man; an idealist and a one-time gambler, he was often described as cold and aloof, obsessed with his own ideas and needs. Living with him, bearing his many children and coping with umpteen pregnancies was not easy for his wife, Sofia, but her midlife crisis, during which she became increasingly desperate and bitter, has always been treated differently from his; while his has been treated with respect, admiration even, as the mark of creative genius, hers has been condemned as a descent into hysteria and insanity. His has been termed a creative crisis, hers a physiological menopausal crisis. Yet both were unhappy, dissatisfied people living a troubled relationship long before they reached midlife.

with them. We all need to eat, for example, and each society teaches its members a set of mores or patterns about eating. But within these patterns each of us eats in a different way and the act of eating has different meanings for different people; some people eat too fast, too much, too little, too often, and so on. Some people spend hours each day thinking about food, others never think about it at all. So even though we all have similar biological pressures (we have to eat), we manage never-theless to evolve our own unique ways of eating and thinking about eating. Similarly, we relate to other people in our own unique ways. We have biological needs to satisfy (for contact, for companionship, for sex, for caring and so on) and we are taught the social forms for expressing these needs, but how we actually do them is unique to us.

As we grow, we evolve our own general patterns of coping with biological and social pressures, and we call these patterns our personalities. And we bring our personalities to every challenge or situation we face; we cope according to the kind of personality we have. So if you're the kind of person that has always reacted badly to physical discomfort, illness or physical change as you were growing up, the chances are you will react in the same way to the changes of midlife. Similarly, if you have coped well with biological changes and illness in the past, you'll not find the midlife challenges as traumatic as might someone else. So if you are used to being self-motivated, if you're confident and essentially a happy person, you might welcome the change that occurs when your children leave home and you have more spare time. But if you've built your personal needs and your security around your children, you might find the changes of the midlife period hard to bear and end up feeling miserable.

What rebelling means

Three sets of overlays interact to produce changes at midlife and it doesn't make much sense to reduce what happens to any one of the overlays. It's much more complicated, but not mysteriously so. Thinking about midlife in terms of these overlays helps us, too, to get a handle on the sense of what we mean by midlife rebellion. Let's consider what rebellion is and see what function it serves in life.

We normally use the term rebellion in the political sense of an insurrection or a reaction against the *status quo*. But in the biological world, rebellion is an *integral* part of survival: when we talk about evolution we automatically invoke a sense of rebellion, especially when we talk about survival of the fittest. What characterizes those who survive in nature? An ability to adjust to change, an ability to move with the herd but to go against the herd when circumstances demand it, to be different. All these characteristics involve the ability to rebel in one way or another.

Think about what we mean when we use the term creativity. Again, the notion of rebellion is involved. We define creativity as an ability to see beyond the *status quo*, an ability to take old forms and to re-make them in new ways, an ability to think for oneself and to be different. Likewise, establishing your own personality involves rebelling. In order to think for yourself you have to rebel to some degree against what you have been told or taught, otherwise we'd all be the same. Think of people who are the mirror-images of their parents or who are dominated by their parents, who can't think for themselves, or stand on their own feet. Nine times out of ten you'll find that they've never been able or allowed to rebel. We admire people who do think for themselves and are capable of being different.

Rebellion is an integral part of biological, social and psychological functioning. And of course there are all sorts of rebellions, good and bad, constructive and destructive. There is a fine line between conforming and rebelling; rebel too much and you'll run into trouble, become an outcast or an eccentric. Taken from this perspective, we can make two points about the role rebellion may have to play in the midlife period.

First, if the ability to rebel is a part of surviving, it follows that there is a good chance that coping with midlife changes will involve having to rebel in one way or another in order to respond effectively to the challenges that come up. We will need therefore to know much more about what constitutes an effective or good midlife rebellion; equally, we will have to know where rebellions can go wrong, can be disguised or misdirected. We'll be looking closely at this in a subsequent chapter.

Secondly, history has taught us (or should have taught us) that we should never ignore or neglect rebellions no matter how pointless we may feel they are or how ineptly they are carried out. There is always something worth noting behind a rebellion, always some issue, some grievance, something of importance that needs our attention and understanding. And the more people try to rebel, the more notice we should take of it. As I have said, we are witnessing a major but relatively silent rebellion by many contemporary midlifers. When so many people challenge the *status quo* it is time to take a long hard look at what lies underneath. We may need to question some of our cherished assumptions about midlife. What I am suggesting here is that the issue of midlife rebellion as it exists in our society today is more than just another rebellion, more than just a reaction to biological changes. It may also be telling us something about our society. I am suggesting in fact that midlife is more significant and more complex than we have realized.

To sum up, popular thinking about midlife appears to have lost track of the fact that life is a complex entity and that at any stage a number of factors determine the pressures we face and the choices we make. In the next three chapters we will look a little closer at each of the overlays we have already outlined. In Chapter Two we'll examine the biology of midlife; in Chapter Three we'll concentrate on the social overlay, the social conditions that help to shape midlife challenges; and in Chapter Four we'll have a look at how individuals shape their own worlds and their own choices.

CHAPTER TWO

The Biology of Midlife

How big a role does biology play in our lives? Are we entirely driven by our biological needs? How much does biology contribute to the changes we experience during the midlife period? These are complicated questions to answer.

What we can do though is focus on the kind of biological factors that are thought to shape what happens to people during midlife and try to clear away some of the confusion that has characterized much of early thinking about midlife. What we need to do in particular is to try and get some idea of what importance we should give to purely biological factors and what weight we should give to the role of social, psychological and environmental influences that also play a part in shaping how we live. First, though, let's establish what we mean when we talk about our biological or physiological natures.

WHAT IS BIOLOGY?

It used to be thought that our biological constitution was a fixed and relatively unchanging entity. When we look at nature, at plants and animals, we see an enormous consistency in the way they grow or behave. We say that their growth or behaviour is biologically determined and there seems little that an animal or plant can do to avoid this fact; the shape they assume and how they grow seems determined by their genes. A leopard never changes its spots. If it ever should, it could only be due to evolution. And when we think of evolution –

21

the most powerful force for change there is in nature – we typically think of it as a large-scale process where any changes occur over thousands or millions of years. We certainly are not used to thinking of nature or evolution as being plastic or pliable and open to environmental pressures. In recent times though research has shown that not only can evolution work much faster than was previously thought, but that social or communal pressures can have marked effects on a range of biological factors including body structure. Even bacteria may have something akin to a social structure in their tiny communities. And we have learnt to our cost how quickly diseases can adjust and change their characteristics to survive the onslaught of antibiotics that have been launched at them over the past half-century. The key words today are change and plasticity.

From this perspective we can see that life for us humans is a matter of living within the framework of two enormously

---

What can social pressure do to fish?

Let us take fish as an example from nature, which are fairly low down on the evolutionary scale. You would imagine that not a lot changes during the life of a single fish, that its physiological structure and its behaviour are mostly predetermined by inherent biological forces. But this is not the case. Things are now known to be a little different. Russell Fernald, a professor of human biology at Stanford University, California, has studied the habits of *Haplochromis Burtoni*, a perch-like fish found in Lake Tanganyika. These fish undergo rather remarkable physiological changes according to their status in the social hierarchy of their fishy world. If you are a powerful top male fish, your colours become brighter, you become sexually potent, and surprisingly, the hypothalamus in your brain – the part that regulates many body functions including endocrine or hormonal functions – becomes bigger. If, however, you lose your position of power, you turn a drab brown colour, you lose your sexual potency and your hypothalamus becomes smaller.

powerful forces – our biological nature, and the actual exigencies that occur in the social world in which we live. Life is a process of gradual momentum, or movement, within the boundaries laid down by the evolutionary process which has set limits to what our musculature and skeletal systems can do. We can't fly like birds or stay underwater like fish; we can't live to be 200 years old. There is however considerable variability within our limits: some of our body organs, such as the heart, are capable of living a lot longer than our bodies as a whole – if only we could work out a way to keep other organs working as well, we could theoretically live for a lot longer. It's been estimated in fact that humans are genetically programmed to live to be about 115 years old. Indeed, certain communities, like those in the Caucasus mountains, seem to have evolved a life-style that helps them, on average, stay alive longer than the rest of us.

So although there are some aspects of our bodies that are determined by our inherited constitution, we can *influence* a great deal. At the simplest level, we can put on or take off

---

Genes and tree-climbing

We can see the interaction between biological and environmental factors very clearly in the way our immune and central nervous systems develop. At birth these systems are pre-programmed in our genes and this ensures that the main structural and functional features of these systems will develop. How well they develop, how they actually function and are structured, depends though on the kind of experience we have as we grow up in contact with the environment. Some parents who are afraid of their children getting diseases may keep them away from contact with other children and not allow them to get dirty, thus limiting the opportunities their children have of developing robust immune systems. Similarly, children who are kept away from physical activity will not learn to develop as well-co-ordinated a central nervous system as children who are encouraged to play ball games, climb trees, and so forth.

weight, or work out in the gym to improve our muscle size, and so make changes within the limits set by our genes. Similarly, biological factors determine our basic needs but much of how we deal with them is dictated by social forces. We are taught when and how to eat and sleep, how to react to fear and anxiety; men and women are taught different ways of coping with and expressing anger not because nature says so, but because society says so.

HORMONAL CHANGES AT MIDLIFE

There are two ways, if you like, that we experience our biological nature. The first is the day-to-day set of cycles or rhythms that govern and regulate our lives. Much of our daily activity is organized around these: we sleep, eat, drink, dream, urinate, make love, have periods, and so on, according to patterns determined by our physiological natures. At this level biological forces are like a low hum in the background that is always there ticking away as time passes; they are so ingrained in our lives we almost forget they are there.

The second way we experience our biological nature comes at certain stages when we begin to notice that we have changed, or are beginning to change, as deeper biological effects kick in over and above the day-to-day pattern. It's as if at key stages the hum gets louder and becomes a roar. The first of the major changes we experience, when biological factors roar loudly in our lives, is due almost entirely to endocrine changes that take place during adolescence. At puberty, previously dormant hormones in males and females become active and set a chain of developmental events into motion. The result is the growth in our bodies we experience as we change from being children to adults and as our gender characteristics become more pronounced. The second major biological change we experience occurs during midlife and is again largely caused by endocrine changes.

Female hormonal changes at midlife

What happens to women during the menopause is that previously active hormones start to reduce their levels of activity and eventually stop altogether. During the earlier part of the menopause (the pre-menopause) the gonadal hormones, oestrogen and progesterone, which regulate the monthly cycle, begin to be secreted in lesser quantities due to the decreasing supply and efficiency of eggs in the ovaries. This causes irregular periods and eventually, during the menopause itself, progesterone secretion stops as the supply of eggs dries up, and oestrogen levels decline, and periods stop altogether.

What is important about the changes in endocrine functioning that mark these major episodes in our lives is that for a number of reasons they can have quite thoroughgoing effects on how our bodies function as a whole. Contrary to popular opinion, the endocrine system does not operate as an independent, self-contained system. The fact that there is a high degree of interaction between the endocrine and other body maintenance systems has important consequences which we need to know about if we are to understand fully the context in which midlife biological changes occur.

The endocrine system is one of the most important of the body's regulatory systems. Along with the nervous and immune systems (with which it is deeply integrated), the endocrine system is responsible for a number of activities ranging from the regulation of internal temperature, blood pressure and metabolic rate to the regulation of growth, sleep and eating cycles and our response to stress. This interaction between the various body maintenance systems helps to explain some of the symptoms and complaints that women voice during the menopause. As hormone levels change in the endocrine system, they interfere with the operation of other systems and apparently strange effects can result as the systems struggle to adjust to the changes.

Don't go away though with the idea that every woman will automatically experience some or all, or indeed any, of the changes listed above. Just as hormonal changes can effect how the body works, so too can the endocrine system be affected by what is going on in other body systems, particularly by what is happening in the central nervous system. The central nervous system – our consciousness – not only allows us to interact with the environment but also largely organizes the internal body hierarchy. It helps to determine the body's state of alertness and arousal, and decides which of the networks in the body has precedence over others.

Hormonal effects

Each of the ovarian hormones has general effects for the whole body as well as for the menstrual cycle; fluctuations in progesterone secretion, for example, can cause mood swings and induce depression. Lack of progesterone has also been linked to the way the body processes some foods (particularly carbohydrates) and some women find their appetites increasing during the menopause. Fluctuations in the secretion level of oestrogen has been similarly linked to widespread changes in several body functions. It has been linked to the loss of elasticity and the increase of dryness in skin, the increase in irritation and acidity in genitourinary skin lining, the loss of power and bulk in muscles, and the loss of fullness in breasts. Oestrogen loss is also involved in the way some foods are processed; menopausal and post-menopausal women are at risk from weakening of the bones due to the fact that oestrogen helps the body process calcium and so less is absorbed after the menopause.

There is another important consequence of the decline in the level of secretion of ovarian hormones. As the supply of these hormones declines in the body, so there is a corresponding change in the overall way the body systems respond to stress. During the menopause, important components of the endocrine response to stress are absent due to the drop in levels of ovarian hormones and therefore the previously established pattern functions differently. What this means is that when you get stressed or upset, your body's cardiovascular and neuroendocrine systems are likely to react differently from in the past. So the ordinary ups and downs of life you used to be able to take in your stride will provoke a more intense or extreme response in your body during the menopause.

If you live under chronic stress and feel that your hold on reality is tentative, you may well find that perfectly normal and ordinary changes in endocrine function are hard to bear precisely because your body is not geared for the changes, or is

Stress and its effects

Stress of any kind can have startling effects on central nervous activity which in turn can interfere with many endocrine functions including the rate at which we grow and the pattern of secretion of hormones, including those that control the menstrual cycle. Stress is a formidable obstacle to normal development and activity; it is well known, for example, that children who grow up in emotionally deprived circumstances can have their growth retarded. Stressful experiences can interfere with the timing of major biological events like adolescence and the menopause; we are all familiar with early or late developers in adolescence, and some cases of premature menopause have been linked to intense psychological or emotional stress.

There are a number of endocrine networks in the body and it seems that when stress disrupts basic rhythms like monthly periods, the stress-response endocrine network takes precedence over networks lower down in the hierarchy.

Stress effects may not always be negative; coping with stress in an active way can take your mind off other body events. Some women, busy managing their worlds, don't even notice the menopause.

not organized for the changes. Since we are each of us unique entities, it follows that we carry different levels of stress and cope with stress in different ways; consequently, how we respond to change will vary, and this goes some way to explaining why some women have a tough time of it during the menopausal years.

Where this is important in our understanding of what happens during the menopause is that it gives us a better idea about the overall biological context in which the purely endocrinological changes occur. If we add to this complexity the fact that different societies teach women different ways of reacting to biological changes, we can see that it is hard to generalize too much about the specific biological effects of the menopause. Each individual's experience is going to be different.

Basic tips on the menopause

- *Get information*: One reason why people with access to information (such as the better educated and the wealthy) get through the menopause more successfully than others is because they are more informed about what is going on and what steps they can take to help themselves. This helps to allay anxiety, makes you feel more in control and genuinely helps you feel better.
- *Adjust to your new rhythms*: The menopause involves changes in biological rhythms. You can help yourself adjust to the physical effects of these by trying the following: change your diet to help your body compensate for the effects of hormone loss, for example by adding calcium. Ensure that you are fit and active so that you're giving your body all the help you can; try to keep your basic rhythms intact. Stay involved with the world around you. Don't collapse or withdraw from life; some studies have found that women who continue to lead an active sexual life suffer less from vaginal dryness than those who avoid sex during the menopause.
- *Build supportive relationships*: Don't forget that women who have a strong and supportive interpersonal network tend to get through the menopause better with fewer problems and symptoms than those who don't have such a support system.
- *Don't be afraid to get help*: If you're struggling, seek help and advice. Try talking to your friends or a doctor. There is so much that can be done these days to ease the symptoms, both emotional and physical, and help you get back on your feet. There's medical help available, counselling, psychotherapy, and so on. People sometimes worry about seeking help from mental health professionals; they fear being labelled insane. However, modern counselling or therapy can help you sort out what's going on in your emotional life and help you cope until you feel better, without ever questioning your sanity.

Hormone Replacement Therapy (HRT)

HRT helps to correct the body's hormonal deficiencies by replacing naturally occurring hormones with manufactured ones. There have been a number of reports favouring their use and they have been shown to reduce many of the symptoms of menopause and to provide protection from some disease risks including bone wasting, stroke and heart attacks. Like most medication though there is also a downside; side effects include nausea and breast tenderness, and there have been reports of an increase in the risk of some forms of cancer (now reduced with broader-spectrum HRT programmes). There is still some controversy about how HRT should be used. Should you use it?

In my opinion there are two points to consider. First, there's nothing wrong with using medication to help you when you're suffering. But sooner rather than later you should get down to sorting out what is going on and find other ways of dealing with it so you don't rely on medication all the time. This applies especially to complex, psychosomatic situations where other emotional or social factors may exist.

Second, we have to bear in mind that there have been many instances in medicine where the tendency to over-medicalize problems has had unfortunate consequences. Remember antibiotics? They were hailed as wonder-drugs and people took them for everything, including the common cold, with the result that the bacteria they were supposed to wipe out simply re-grouped and evolved more resistant strains, thus weakening the power of the antibiotics. Remember some of the tranquillizers that were given out like sweets until it was realized that they often created as many problems as they solved? I suspect that there is a danger that hormone replacement treatments may in time fall into the same category as antibiotics and tranquillizers if they are over-used or seen as a 'cure-all'. HRT should therefore be used carefully and in context.

at is common to all women though is the fact that sooner or later things change biologically during midlife. The key word here is *change*. Suddenly your biological nature roars again, just as in adolescence. After years of living with the hormonal patterns of a woman, during the menopause you end up having to live with the kind of hormonal levels that men have. This is a major change, but it's one that can be survived. It's not as if your body is suddenly deprived of all hormones (for example, your body continues to make some oestrogen in cell tissue) or that your endocrine system closes down for good. The difficulty is that after years of living with a relatively stable level of body functioning, you have to adjust to a new challenge; you have to re-learn, as it were, a new set of ways of dealing with your body. If you can remember your adolescence you'll probably remember what it was like.

Male hormonal changes at midlife

What happens to men's hormones during midlife? The hormonal cycle plays a much greater role in a woman's life physically, emotionally and psychologically than it does in a man's, and male hormonal activity changes very little throughout a man's lifetime. Unlike women, men remain fertile until death. However, it is popularly believed that male hormonal secretions, like those of women, gradually decrease with age and this has been linked to the so-called male menopause. The prime causes according to this view are the male androgen hormones, a falling secretion of which, it has been argued, is in some way linked to the sexual difficulties traditionally associated with the male climacteric.

There have undoubtedly been reports of sexual difficulties associated with ageing, but little really clear evidence that this is due to a failure in hormonal activity. Certainly there appears to be a biological change in these hormones with ageing, but the studies show that any changes seem to be relatively minor compared to the hormonal changes menopausal women experience. Studies have found a decline in some measures of hormonal activity with age, particularly a decline in androgen levels, but there is wide variability between individuals and no clear relationship between this decline and the sexual difficulties associated with ageing in men. The most commonly mentioned complaints are a loss of sexual appetite and impotence amongst older men, but this is by no means widespread; there have been some studies that have shown that an important percentage of men even display an increase in their sexual desire and behaviour as they age. There is general agreement that any hormonal changes that do occur are to be found amongst elderly men, not amongst men in the middle years of their lives.

Most researchers agree that the sexual difficulties described by older men are not related to hormonal changes but are rather confined to a group of men with specific histories of psychological problems and certain medical problems including high blood pressure, heart disease and diabetes, all of which are known to produce some of the effects attributed to hormonal changes. Smoking, excessive preoccupation with career, excessive drinking and overeating are believed to play a significant role in the development of many of the complaints about sexual feelings and performance in older men. Since these factors can also influence sexual performance at any age, we can hardly regard them as biological.

THE EFFECTS OF AGEING

From approximately 20 years of age onwards, we don't grow much: our muscular-skeletal systems remain fairly static. This does not mean that growth or change as such stops; we continue to change but in a more subtle way. Most of our body maintenance and regulatory systems are in place and will continue to function until we die – subject to disease or accident. Our skin will continue to grow and replace damaged areas, our immune system will continue to fight off invaders and our endocrine system will help us to maintain a relatively stable level of body function. Our major organs will continue to keep things ticking over. Slowly, very slowly, they will decay with age, but the rate at which they do so will depend on the kind of life-events that we experience and the kind of personality we have: in other words, on the way we use or abuse our bodies.

Much of what people think of as ageing has to do with appearance and behaviour. We see young people, active, fit, sleek, slim, full of energy; they look good. Ageing seems to mean loss of looks, and loss of energy and vigour. Many other contemporary beliefs back up the notion of a continuum. We talk for example about people peaking in intelligence and creativity in their young years; we talk about having your best ideas before you're 25; after 30 we talk about being over the hill.

The fact that ageing brings with it an increased risk of falling ill from one of the chronic diseases is yet another sign of this biological process at work. Read any book on midlife and its crises and you'll find an almost overwhelming focus on dealing with the biological decay thought to be involved in the ageing process: how to hide the signs of ageing; how to boost flagging sexual drive; how to cope with menopausal difficulties and so on. There's rarely a mention of the biological *challenges* involved.

Fortunately we now know a great deal more about the way the body ages. There are a number of basic, biologically determined ageing factors that will begin to show as you reach middle age and beyond. External skin will dry out, loosen, line and wrinkle; hair-loss may occur; teeth will sooner or later loosen; eyesight may suffer. These are basics in that everyone sooner or later will be affected by them but not necessarily at the same rate or the same time. Ageing means the passage of time; it may involve decay but it can also involve growth; you can develop new skills at any time in your life.

Thinking skills

There are certain aspects of cognitive functioning that are traditionally believed to deteriorate with age, in particular memory and intelligence. It is believed for example that as you age your thinking slows down, your memory begins to go and you find it harder to learn new skills. Again, the question we need to ask, if this is true, is how much is this a function of inherited biological factors and how much is it due to other, non-biological factors?

Certainly cognitive function *changes* with age. If you compare the performances of elderly people to those of young adults on most cognitive tasks, you will find that older people don't perform on average as well as young ones do. However, while some of this fall-off in cognitive ability may be due to biological changes associated with ageing (for example, neuronal loss in the central nervous system), most of the change seems to be

Some basic tips

- Face up to ageing by taking it as a challenge; don't try to ignore it and don't try to hide it. We'd all cope with ageing better if we stopped seeing it as a bad, ugly or generally undesirable state. People's attitudes determine these feelings, not the ageing process.

- Keeping your body in a healthy state is a matter of common sense; you should try to keep relatively fit and active; you should try to eat a balanced diet and avoid being over- or under-weight. Keeping fit not only keeps your body systems in an efficient state but it can help to slow down the onset of the muscle wasting and joint stiffness associated with old age. Studies in the United States have found that elderly people who run regularly or do aerobic exercises tend to die older and to suffer fewer disabilities.

- Learn how to minimize stress where possible and learn to cope with it in healthy ways; reduce risky habits like smoking, excessive intake of alcohol, food or drugs. If you can't change on your own, don't be afraid or too proud to get help from friends or a professional.

- Above all try to keep your basic skills alive. Don't stop thinking, relating, trying new things just because you're old. Remember: physical and mental mobility is the key. One of the best examples of someone who never stopped using his mental skills was Linus Pauling the double Nobel Prize winner; he was still thinking, still turning his mind to new skills right up until he died at the age of 93. Another good example is Mrs Bandaranaike (79), the Sri Lankan politician who was the first female prime minister in the world and who has just started a new job as President of her country.

- Work at preserving yourself. Look good by all means, but do it in a healthy way, that is, for yourself, not for what other people will think of you or your looks.

due to other factors, not connected with biological factors. Younger people are often capable of performing better at routine tasks because they are capable of intense focusing and don't bring to the task the kind of emotional clutter (and other worries) that older people do. Younger people often have an intense drive to prove themselves which older, calmer people don't feel. A lot also depends on the kinds of skills measured. While young people do well on simple, straightforward tasks, older people seem to be able to think more broadly, to take a range of factors into account in solving problems, and to be able to juggle with a number of conflicting factors at the same time. Older people are often calmer too in their thinking. Perhaps the best proof of this is Nasa's astronaut training programme; many of the astronauts are middle-aged, experienced people, chosen for their ability to stay calm and thoughtful under stress.

For a variety of reasons older people neglect their thinking skills; they simply don't get the opportunity to try new things or to keep old learning skills alive. One thing that can happen as we age is that we may get trapped in relatively static ways of thinking. We forget how to tackle and learn new things, we get staid, set in our ways. We also get scared of change. New tasks threaten our status in ways that don't threaten a younger person. We forget that to keep our minds active we need to keep learning, to keep accepting challenges.

Another problem is that as people age they may withdraw into their most comfortable relationships and avoid meeting new people and confronting new situations, with the result that they neglect their cognitive and relating skills. People who don't do this, who keep their minds open to new challenges and new experiences, inevitably are able to retain high levels of cognitive functioning.

Disease

One other factor that we need to consider with respect to midlife is the role that disease plays. We know that people over the age of 40 become increasingly prone to some diseases, particularly heart disease and cancer. Can this have some bearing on midlife problems?

Well, yes, obviously it can. If you suffer from a disease,

everything becomes much harder. There is the effect of the disease on your body; no one performs at their best when they are suffering from pain and discomfort or if they are taking medication or undergoing other forms of medical treatment. Being ill also places a tremendous emotional strain on the person which can have important somatic consequences; fear and anxiety can make it very hard to cope with the 'normal' stresses and changes of the midlife period. Having an ill person in a family can also create problems for the rest of the family.

It is important though to realize that the tendency for people over 40 to be more prone to disease than younger people is not strictly a biological part of midlife in the same way, for example, that we can talk of endocrine changes as being an inherent, genetically determined event. Most of the diseases that emerge at midlife or later are chronic diseases caused by a number of factors that require time for their effects to become manifest. They have a lot to do with life-style choices as much as with organic problems. As we've said, theoretically, the body can go on a lot longer than the three score years and ten. The killer modern diseases take time to build up their effects; that they coincide with the midlife period is not a biological fact but has a lot to do with what has happened earlier in life. Diseases like cancer and heart conditions rarely *start* in midlife. They start in young adulthood and they *show up* in midlife. What the biological changes of midlife can do though, especially in women, is to increase the *rate* at which these diseases show. We noted earlier, for example, that women during the menopause may experience a general increase in their cardiovascular and neuroendocrinal responses to stress, and it follows therefore that these increased reactions may well make a pre-established heart condition worse or speed up the development of a pre-existing tumour such as breast cancer.

There are other disease risks though that are to do with ageing. As we mentioned earlier, menopausal and post-menopausal women may run the risk of developing diseases that follow on from changes in their hormonal functioning. One such disease is osteoporosis, a condition of low bone density which may in part be caused by falling oestrogen levels. However, some of the diseases that we have traditionally associated with ageing have now been shown to need more complex explanations. Osteoarthritis, a cartilage disease and the most common form of arthritis, was for years believed to be a part of the ageing process. It was thought – indeed still is thought – that this was due to a gradual wearing down with age (and use) of weight-bearing joints in the body. However, research has established that only about 50% of older people suffer from this and that it can occur in young people.

We also associate ageing with the loss of efficiency of our immune systems and the gradual wearing-out of the major organs, but it is now thought that this has less to do with ageing and more to do with a range of life-style factors. Much the same can be said of a variety of other body troubles that have usually been associated with ageing, such as insomnia, loss of appetite (sexual and otherwise) and loss of drive. It now seems clear that these can occur in all age groups and there seems to be little evidence to suggest that they are associated purely with the ageing process.

| THE KEY ISSUE | *Coping with the changes* |

To summarize, there are biological changes that accompany midlife and help to make the period a notable one. Equally, as we have seen, it is all too easy to focus on these changes and see the problems, challenges and crises of midlife as being essentially biological in nature. Unfortunately we live in a society that likes to put people into broad and superficial categories, and nowhere is this more apparent than in how we categorize people according to age. These categories help enormously to strengthen the notion that we are uniform entities – that what is happening to one person in the category is happening in the same way to everyone else in the category. Equally midlife has become a convenient basket in which to toss (and explain) a complex and varied web of experience. It makes it easy to think of midlife as a convenient biological stage just like adolescence and old age, and this obscures the enormously complex relationships that exist between biology, society and individual psychology.

We must be careful not to lay the blame for midlife problems solely at the door of the biological changes that occur. What seems to be much more important is how we react to these changes, how we cope with them and what they mean to us.

Just as the biological changes of adolescence create major development tasks for teenagers, so the biological changes of midlife should be seen as presenting important developmental tasks for middle-aged people.

Midlife changes can shake our subjective worlds, and the real task is to rebel effectively against both our own tendency to ignore our biology and against the simplistic ways that our society teaches us to think about midlife. Of course we can hide the effects of ageing to some degree in order to continue to keep our subjective view of ourselves stable for a time. It makes much more sense however to get a better grasp of what's going on in ourselves, re-evaluate our old securities (and vanities) and to try to find a healthier way of rebelling against that of which we are afraid – ageing and death and time running out before we have achieved what we want for ourselves. The changes of the menopause, the changes that ageing brings and the increased risk of diseases are all challenges to be faced, not by patching things up or glossing over the issues so that we can carry on as before, but by using the opportunity to have a good look at ourselves, our bodies and how we cope with them.

CHAPTER THREE

Why Things are Different Now

Just as the biological clock that beats away inside our bodies helps to shape what happens to us in life, so too does the social world exert its own demands and pressures. If we look at some of the political, social and economic changes that have taken place in our society over the past two centuries, we see that some of the pressures we experience in midlife are in part due to these upheavals. We can start by sketching the general features of the changes that have taken place and then have a closer look at what has happened in the period since the end of the Second World War.

AFTER THE REVOLUTION(S)

Economic and political events are the two important forces that shape social values and at the same time define life for the ordinary person, and this has been especially true in the modern period of history. We have seen industrial and techno-logical revolutions, a shift from an agriculture-based economy to an industry-based one, huge movements of populations from the country to towns, and we have seen our cities grow to unimaginable sizes. We have seen science and medicine grow in importance and seen changes in our living standards, our health standards and in the kinds of diseases we face. We have seen world wars, the democratization of political and social institutions, the advent of new forms of communication and changes in how we spend our spare time. All of these events have had an effect on the way our society works and on the kinds of pressure ordinary people have had to face.

These events have affected the way we live and the quality of life we experience. Life for the vast majority of people in the 19th century and for much of the 20th century was very much a matter of staving off hunger and disease, surviving warfare and trying to cope with the upheavals of the industrial revolution. The life expectancy of the average person in the 19th century was much lower than it is today. Times were hard, diets were poor, living and hygiene conditions were inadequate. Opportunities for change were few and far between. You lived your life within the narrow confines of physical geography, social class and your economic circumstances. Social and political pressures locked you in place and religious beliefs ensured that you stayed locked, that you accepted your lot in life.

There was little room for psychological or emotional considerations in a world marked by more physical concerns. There was also no one to listen to you even if you did voice emotional problems or difficulties; if anyone found life too much to bear there was always the asylum waiting if things got out of hand. Within this framework, midlife had a very narrow meaning for most men and women. For a woman, in those days before contraception and in the days of relatively primitive birth conditions, the menopause often meant freedom from repeated pregnancies and pain and discomfort. But it also marked the closing in of life; few women lived for very long after the midlife period. For a man, if he reached the age of 40 he probably considered himself lucky to have survived for so long in one piece.

Not surprisingly things were different for the wealthy. There was time to think, there was freedom from the immediate cares and concerns that defined reality for the poor. Moreover, there was the financial means and confidence to do something about problems or discomforts that arose. Having wealth meant that, if you so chose, you could be spared the problems of raising a family and coping with children; you could always employ nannies and servants to take care of the drudgery and leave you free to get on with other things. Wealthy women in midlife could afford to pay to see the likes of Dr Tilt and to spend six months on one of his cures; wealthy men could afford to keep a mistress or modify their life-styles to accommodate any midlife troubles they were experiencing.

While we have seen devastating wars and economic

hardships in the 20th century, slowly but surely the lot of the ordinary person has changed. Standards of living have risen; education, health care and diets have changed for the better and the rights of ordinary people have gradually been improved. The average life-span has increased. There are now more old people proportionately in the general population than ever before, and this will increase in time. More people than ever reach the midlife period and they can expect to live well into old age.

The pace of these improvements has increased significantly after 1950. If we look at the economic and political events that have occurred in the period since the end of the Second World War, we see that it has been a period of relative peace and considerable economic growth. There have been wars (Korea, Vietnam) and economic hardships (unemployment and stockmarket crashes) but ordinary people have been insulated from the worst effects of these events by the fact that wars took place far away, often on the other side of the world, and by the advent of the welfare state.

The introduction of the welfare state after the Second World War brought with it vast improvements in the basic living standards of most people: improved nutrition and health care, better education, unemployment benefits, housing, social and legal benefits and so on. Money supply improved and gradually living standards rose. Television introduced a new leisure activity into the home.

These social and economic changes have brought with them many benefits. They have meant that children nowadays grow

---

Life expectancy

In the 19th century, average life expectancy in Britain was under 45 years; today it is over 70 and getting higher. In Japan, which has the best record in this respect of all industrialized societies, it's higher still. Japanese men have a life expectancy of 76 years, women 82 years. In terms of pure survival, midlife has become much more important simply because there is now almost as much time to live after the midlife period as before it.

up healthier and better educated, and free to a large extent from the anxieties of people growing up in the 19th century or in the first half of the 20th century. For the first time ever, millions of ordinary people, not just the wealthy, have been free to think about matters other than the pressing needs of basic survival. But there have been other, more subtle, consequences.

Changes in the family

One of the effects of the industrial revolution was that it altered the size and constitution of the average family. Prior to the industrial revolution, you could find quite a variety of families including the nuclear family (similar to our basic family today but usually with more children), the extended family in which two or more generations lived under the same roof, and the semi-extended family in which members of the same extended family, while not necessarily sharing the same roof, nevertheless lived in close proximity to one another. In rural areas and even in industrialized towns, the extended family and the semi-extended family were the established mode of family life. In some communities the extended family was the basic economic unit of the community, just as they are today in those cultures that have not experienced the industrial revolution.

With the advent of the industrial revolution, extended families gradually broke up as people drifted to where they could find work – in the cities and factories. Over time, even the semi-extended family slowly disappeared to be replaced by the nuclear family that we are familiar with today, consisting of the husband, wife and children. A generation or two back, family members still tended to stay fairly close to one another and often played quite important roles in one another's lives. Nowadays, adult children are encouraged to get right away from home and stand on their own feet as soon as their education is finished. Improved economic circumstances have made it possible for many young couples to move into their own homes much earlier than in the past, rather than have to spend time living with their parents.

There has also been a change in the size of families. We have fewer children now than people did earlier in the 20th century or the 19th century. One of the results of this change in the family structure has been that children now tend to be born fairly close together, often in their parents' early twenties, and reach adolescence and adulthood at about the time when their parents enter the midlife period.

These changes have made a difference to the pattern of our home lives and our relationships within the family. More important for us here, they have helped to create a set of pressures and changes at or around the midlife period in novel ways that by and large were not present as intensely in previous generations.

You can see this most clearly if you think about the effect on a mother of having only two children born relatively closely together (the way things are now) as compared to a mother earlier in the 20th century who may have had anything up to six or eight children to care for. Whereas the latter frequently had to contend with a lifetime of child rearing, the modern mother now has a natural break occurring when her children leave home during her midlife period. Naturally this change also affects the father but most women still take more responsibility for child rearing than men do. For a woman who has lived her life through her role as a mother, poured all her energies into child rearing, this natural break can come as a major challenge. In fact it's even got a name – the empty nest syndrome – and it can cause emotional difficulties depending on a number of factors including the strength of the parental relationship and the smoothness and ease with which the children leave home. By the same token, a woman trying to juggle a home, a career and children can suddenly find herself freed of at least one set of responsibilities when her children leave home and she can then get on with whatever she wants to do.

The emergence of adolescence

Another important and often neglected consequence of these changes in family life has been the emergence of the notion of adolescence as a significant and sometimes problematic period, particularly since the end of the Second World War. While adolescence has always been a feature of growing up, there have been changes in the way children are treated and educated during adolescence. Earlier in the 20th century, children of 13 or 14 were expected to leave school and go out to work. It was the relatively wealthy or gifted few that stayed on at school. Today children have to stay at school well into their adolescence and in doing so remain dependent on their parents, having marginal status for far longer than previously. It is this extended period of dependence and marginality that is usually cited as the reason adolescent problems have become so important.

The emergence of adolescence as an issue is important for our consideration of what pressures arise during midlife, because as children go through their adolescence they inevitably come into conflict with those in authority. In days gone by this burst of rebellious fervour was often dissipated by the demands of working and earning a living, and any left-over conflict was most likely to be shared by the parents, members of the extended family, the boss, and so on. These days most of this energy is focused undiluted on parents and teachers – those who have the most contact with them. For the average parent, coping with adolescent problems can be a fairly traumatic and troubling task, as we shall see in a later chapter. What we need to appreciate at this point is that these problems usually emerge in late adolescence when the parents are about to enter midlife or are already in it. And again, let us not forget that the parent most likely to have to face the brunt of these challenges to their authority and personality is the mother. Perhaps this is why women who don't have children are reported to have an easier menopause!

Elderly parents

In earlier times it was customary to stay close to one's own parents even if you left home, but it has now become the norm for children to move away and distance themselves from their parents. Elderly parents who have been independent and self-sufficient for years may suddenly need help if their circumstances change, and this can create pressure or problems for their middle-aged children. It's not at all unusual for elderly parents in these circumstances to make a re-appearance in family life after years of living in the background. Suddenly you have to think about another person's needs and demands, a person with whom you have had a long relationship that may well need reworking and re-examining from a new perspective. You may find yourself in the position of being depended upon rather than the other way around.

THE CURRENT GENERATION

Two factors serve to distinguish the present generation from those previous. It is the first generation to have grown up during an era in which many of the hopes and ideals of the modern period of history have come to fruition. It has been an era of relative peace and economic prosperity. It does, at least superficially, look as if the aims and promises of scientific rationalism – the notion that we can progress to a rational and objective social system – have been shown to be attainable. Certainly people growing up during this period have been educated to believe so.

The second point is the rather more obvious one that since many of the basic needs of members of the community have been taken care of, there have been more opportunities and much more time to explore other aspects of life and living. We have, for example, developed a much broader consciousness about the quality of our lives. We have become more concerned, for example, about our health, paying attention to our diets and to staying fit. As we have seen, there has also been a tremendous growth in interest in inner states: psychological, emotional and spiritual.

This spirit of concern about the quality of our lives has created a climate in which we automatically expect these aspects to be important and to be dealt with. Middle-aged people of today have been the first generation to be reared on these expectations and it should come as no surprise that a generation so reared should begin to voice similar concerns about the midlife period. They have been taught to expect ideals and dreams to come true, and at midlife they expect to have their concerns, emotions and inner feelings recognized and attended to just as they have in the past.

This I think is one of the most important reasons why the present midlife generation is so different and why so many of them are experiencing a kind of 'What's happening to me?' crisis. When you grow up with so many benefits and expect to have your feelings and ideas attended to, it can come as a shock to find yourself marginalized and unattended to, and fobbed off with beliefs and ideas that are half a century out of date.

The mind industry

From the cradle to the grave we are fascinated by what goes on inside the minds of people. We even study the brain waves of foetuses in the womb and worry about what effects our life-styles have on the developing foetus. There has been an enormous amount of attention focused on the developmental and learning experience of our children. Sixty years ago you were told what to learn and you got on with it; no one was interested in your emotional state – whether or not the teaching system worked for you. If you had problems at school it was your affair; you coped as best you could. Today we worry about whether or not we are good parents and about whether or not we are harming our children. If you had a difficult adolescence, if you have an unhappy relationship – if, in fact, you have any psychological or emotional problem – there is a place for it in modern society. And there is a whole army of professionals available to back these new interests up: psychologists, social workers, journalists, and so on.

The right to rebel

Quite apart from the benefits and changes discussed above, there have been two important social movements during the past few decades which many present-day middle-aged people have taken part in. The one movement has been broadly concerned with the general rights of people and the rights of marginal and minority groups. Society has had to re-assess its ways of dealing with and giving status to traditionally under-privileged or neglected people. Women for example got the right to vote in Britain after the First World War, but it was only with the rise of the women's movement that the right of women to participate fully in society became – and remains – a pressing issue. The rights of children have changed radically to the extent that we are presently debating the right of parents to smack their children: in Sweden it is against the law to do so. We have also seen in recent times a change in the rights of minority groups to live and work in a society without any discrimination on racial, religious or sexual grounds. While we are nowhere near achieving full equality – some would say that we have barely begun to work at these issues – the fact is that the right to challenge tradition is now well established. The right to query the *status quo* has become a part of our lives.

What is important about these changes is that they have been achieved (if one can use that word) through social action. By and large no government and no legal system has automatically given rights to the people concerned – they were achieved by questioning the existing system and by concerned people actively *rebelling* against tradition. Think of the suffragette movement in Britain in the early 20th century when women went out and chained themselves to railings or threw themselves under racehorses to get their views heard; think of strikes and protests and demonstrations – not just those of more recent history but those earlier in the century. In many ways the 20th has been a century of rebellion against tradition. In fact, if you look back over the past two hundred years, much of the progress that has been made has been achieved by rebellion. The American revolution, the French revolution, the industrial revolution, the Russian revolution: things have changed through revolution and conflict with the powers-that-be.

One important consequence of developments such as these has been a change in the social definition of rebellion. If you raise people on philosophies of change through rational and scientific progression, if you provide massive evidence of how things can change, and if you provide information about how other people live so that the perspective of the ordinary person broadens, then sooner or later people begin to think it perfectly natural to ask radical or revolutionary questions about the nature of their societies. The developments we discussed above reflect this new definition, but in addition there has been a second social movement that has grounded this new concept of rebellion at a more personal level.

The Woodstock generation

Already by the 1950s and early 1960s there were signs that people were beginning to ask searching questions about the traditional way they were expected to live their private lives. The beatniks of the beat generation were one of the earliest groups to actively rebel against the established order that specified, amongst other things, how you dressed, how you behaved, how you thought and how you related. However, it was the social and political upheavals of the late 1960s and early 1970s that gave impetus to the notion that if you wanted to change things you had to rebel openly and take part personally.

There were important political aims to what we can call the general upheavals of the 1960s and 1970s. Much of the political action was aimed at breaking the hold and the ideologies of traditional groups that held power in government, in the media and in education. But for the ordinary person they were an attempt to break down centuries-old ways of thinking about personal morality and relationships that no longer served the needs of people reared under different circumstances. You might like to remember just how much of a hold these old standards had over our lives. What we saw, heard or read in the media was severely censored. Individuality and talent went unrecognized because of how you looked, how you talked, how long your hair was. There was tremendous emphasis on conformity: you could dress in any colour you wanted so long as it was drab. You could relate anyway you liked so long as it was conventional.

Quite apart from the fact that those revolutionary movements involved more people in the act of rebelling and questioned a greater range of social mores than ever before, the people who took part learnt one very important lesson – that things could be done, that things could change. You were not automatically bound by existing traditions, you could do things differently if you wanted to or had the courage to do so. This therefore was a generation with *personal* experience of revolution; this was not a rebellion by a minority group or a political group, it was a mass, across-the-board, popular revolution.

This is a key point. As we've said, in the past, rebellion was often associated with extreme movements or with eccentricity, both of which put you outside the range of 'normal' society or made you an outcast. The revolutions of the 1960s and 1970s occurred *within* society, and society eventually adjusted to the challenges. A modern-day Gauguin would be lost in the crowd. Most young people growing up through those times developed a belief in personal power, that they could change social institutions through rebelling rather than through conforming. Encouraged by these achievements, people applied the same rationale to more personal issues: their relationships, careers and their ideas of personal fulfilment. These values were in almost complete contrast to those of the preceding generation who were the ones the young people rebelled against.

| THE KEY ISSUE | *The fight goes on* |

What has happened to the young adults of the Woodstock generation as they have progressed to midlife? Did things turn out as they had expected? Are they satisfied with what they see around them?

It seems to me that by and large the answer to both these questions is No. The hopes and dreams of the Woodstock generation have not been fulfilled. While society has become in many ways more open, more accepting of individual differences than in the past, many middle-aged people of today feel that little else has changed. When they stand back and look at what has happened in society they feel disappointed.

Much of the discontent they feel is expressed as a frustration with the slowness of political and social change. Some feel that in many ways the clock has been put back, that inequalities and injustices still abound and in some instances things are even worse than they were before. Others feel that their faith in science and political philosophies has been shaken. Science, some of them say, has sold out to big business, and most of the political ardour and conviction they felt in their youth has led nowhere as the institutions and parties they supported have diluted their programmes.

By far the greatest dissatisfaction, though, is expressed as frustration with the way that their hopes for better personal relationships has turned out. The morals revolution was a reaction in part to the way society had traditionally said that relationships were to be conducted. People wanted more freedom to explore their needs and particularly their sexual and emotional needs. They no longer wanted to wait until they were married to experience intimacy, and they wanted the freedom to get out of a relationship if they no longer wanted to stay in. But the morals revolution was also about greater freedom to explore yourself and to become the person that you wanted without being restricted by gender or class or even hair length. It was about finding yourself.

The difficulty has been that while there was a rebellion against convention, little real thought was given to the underlying nature of the problems posed by living in relationships in society. It was believed that living a more open and freer existence – in short, rebelling against the old school – was enough. The morals revolution opened up issues, asked questions, exposed weaknesses in the existing framework, but didn't solve them. Slogans such as free love, brotherhood and sisterhood, and so on, sounded fine at the time, but in fact were essentially meaningless as practical solutions to the difficulties relationships pose.

Personal relationships are the most complex forms of human interaction. They are also the bedrock on which the economic and social institutions of our society are based; our society is structured around the couple and the family. And these structures in turn create enormous pressures to conform to social expectations. The ideals of the morals revolution quickly came up against the institutionalized reality of our societies, and conflict was inevitable.

To take one example: open relationships involved, in theory, people being free to experiment and explore their personalities in relationships which they could enter or leave far more easily than in the past. In practice, this tended to mean sexual experiment and exploration but with very little emotional and personal exploration. The theory demanded equality – in fact preached it – between partners: equal freedom, equal rights and responsibilities, equal opportunities. But the reality was very different. Society made no real attempt to resolve the problems created by the new ideas and the demands of reality; women still had babies, relationships still needed a set form even if some women now had careers and a life of their own. Society has remained male-orientated in the sense that industry still prefers to employ males and the worlds of art, music and the media remain male-dominated to this day. And there has been no significant attempt to cater for the special needs of working mothers. This pattern can be found throughout our society, in homes, for example, despite all that you hear about the new dispensation, studies have shown that less than 5% of households share family chores; most women continue in their traditional roles of home-makers and child-rearers.

Despite all this, many current midlifers are still in a sense waging war against convention. We are in fact at a very important point in the evolution of our society. We are, I think, seeing for the first time some of the deeper ramifications of the social and economic changes that have occurred during the 20th century. The present midlife generation has been raised under different conditions, both materially and psychologically, from previous generations and their expectations are different. They are used to thinking critically, and many of them are used to rebelling and taking matters into their own hands. While some middle-aged people are frustrated and despondent about their lives, large numbers are still out there, busy redefining all previous interpretations of the midlife period.

Single parents

One new phenomenon that has arisen in this generation is that of the single parent. More families today are run by one parent – usually a woman – than ever before. For some people this is taken as evidence that the morals revolution has fizzled out at the social level. Take Margaret for example: 'When I compare myself to my mother I want to weep. When I was in my twenties I used to think she was a real victim of her time – the conventional middle-aged woman in her tweeds, browbeaten into conforming to a conventional life. I vowed then that it wouldn't happen to me. I was a real rebel. I was a hippy and all the rest. I believed things would be different by the time I became middle-aged. Well they're not. It's worse. My mother at least has room and time to move. I'm completely trapped. I work and then I rush home to take care of my kids. It's like having two jobs. I have no time for anything else. I feel crushed.'

Other people though feel that it is a change for the better in that it has allowed them to get out of unhappy situations that they might have otherwise stayed in. Either way, one thing is certain: this change in family structure has created another new situation for many midlifers to confront.

Unlike the present-day younger generation, which seems to have other preoccupations, middle-aged people now appear determined to carry through their rebellious activities at the personal level. Thwarted by society, they are engaging in a quieter, more personal form of rebellion. They are exploring relationships and exploring their emotional and spiritual needs, still trying to find themselves. They know they have many years still to live and they want to live them out trying to fulfil their dreams. I think that more than anything else it is this desire to fulfil their dreams that marks them off from previous generations. Previous generations were urged to give up their dreams when they reached midlife. Nowadays many 40- or 50-year-olds are hell-bent on being dragged out still trying to live life to the full!

To summarize, we now have some idea how social and economic forces help to shape what happens during the midlife period, and we have seen how these factors have helped to create a period of life in which several sets of challenges come together. Each generation has to face its own set of challenges and we have now some insight into the kind of problems and challenges that our generation of middle-aged people has to face. Again, the key issue is coping with change. There are changes in social and family circumstances to face; there may be more time to focus on yourself, a slackening of pressure, opportunity for thinking and doing.

CHAPTER FOUR

Individuality

We have looked so far at the biological factors that drive our lives and we've seen how the social world in which we live is responsible for some of the changes that occur during the midlife period. Despite the enormous power and influence of these forces, on their own they don't fully account for what happens during midlife. Even though we all share a common biological inheritance and we are raised in a common social and cultural framework, each one of us grows up to be an individual, unique in the way we experience and see life and how we cope with its problems. It is this individuality that gives the final shape to what happens to us during midlife.

What does this mean for our understanding of the midlife period? There are several ways that who or what we are as individuals can help shape midlife experience. If you've had a hard, stressed or unhappy life, for example, you might find coping with midlife challenges just one challenge too many to bear. Similarly, if you're vulnerable to biological changes, coping with midlife changes can be especially difficult; or, if several sets of unfortunate circumstances coincide with the midlife period as sometimes happens, then midlife and its changes can make your life seem like hell. However, events such as these may *coincide* with midlife but not necessarily be part of the midlife process; they can happen at other times too with just as miserable or unfortunate consequences. It's chance or fate, in a way, and by the same token good things can happen to individuals at midlife or at any other time.

There are two basic ways that our individual natures influence what can happen during the midlife period. The first is concerned with how we cope with stress and change, and the second is concerned with the development of our sense of individuality.

HOW YOU COPE MATTERS

Some of midlife's changes are outside our control and have little to do with our individuality; we can't stop our biological clocks nor can we easily change the social circumstances in which we live. But what *is* under our control is how we cope with these changes. We know that some people cope with the challenges of midlife really well. We also know that not all unhappy or unlucky people collapse at midlife. Some people thrive on stress and challenge. So, we need to know what it is about who we are as individuals that can make the difference between coping and not coping with midlife.

Most of us have at least a rough idea of what it means to cope. It means getting by without collapsing or causing too much trouble or being a nuisance. Society admires people who cope or who don't rock the boat or cause a fuss, and each one of us grows up to some extent equipped with a set of 'approved' coping methods which we use to manage the ups and downs of life. It is left to our families to 'fine tune' this set of expectancies and to ensure that each individual, each growing child, learns to fit into the social pattern. It is here, in the family, that things can go astray.

Why are we different

At birth we are almost pure individuals, more so than at any time of our lives. Babies are entirely self-focused with practically no awareness of anyone or anything else around them. They are concerned simply with trying to get their needs attended to as quickly as possible, preferably instantly.

What saves us from growing up to be entirely self-centred individuals is the fact that there are a number of people around us determined to change this and turn us into social beings, capable of living in communities. From day one of our lives we engage in a constant battle between our own inbuilt wilfulness and the social pressures we have to contend with; our own

individuality emerges as we strive to maintain a balance between what we want and what others want from us. We learn
to compromise, to rebel, to fight, to submit and as we do so we
create our own ways of coping.

Our individuality doesn't emerge out of thin air; we are
taught by our parents and we copy their ideas about coping,
but we also evolve our own style within this framework. Our
parents are the first to stand in the way of our childhood need
for instant gratification; they stop us from doing what we want
or giving us what we want immediately. They guide and teach
by blocking us, channelling our needs into acceptable social
avenues of gratification. This first 'conflict' between what we
want and what they want contains the seeds of the later development of our own individuality. How we solve this early conflict, and how we adjust to it, lays the foundation for how we
cope with most later challenges.

To survive you have to be different

There is an important principle involved here. While the child
soon learns that it is practically helpless without its parents and
that they are the most powerful creatures in its world, so too
does it begin to realize that there are limits to the power that
parents hold and this creates something of a dilemma. The
parents do control the child in very large part, and very early
on the child learns that life can be a lot easier if it does what
these powerful people want. However, there are very real
limits to this power. First, the parents cannot control everything that happens to the child, so there are areas of freedom
in which the child is left to his or her own devices. Second, the
parents can't be there all the time and the child has to solve
problems and manage fears or anxieties on its own.

To cope with these limits of parental power the child slowly
learns to internalize parental instructions. Sometimes these
work. Sometimes they don't. Sometimes the parents have got
it wrong (they may have given the wrong advice or no advice).
Sometimes the child gets it wrong (it may misunderstand the
parents' commands). Either way, the child soon learns that
there are holes, gaps, weaknesses or blank spots that it has to
fill in for itself. Sooner or later the child realizes that its survival
depends on being able to think and act for itself almost as much

as on listening to its parents. In order to fill the gaps in its parents' system the child has to develop its own set of commands, and its map of reality usually incorporates a relatively strong or weak role for its own contribution.

There is more than just a question of being different involved in this process. If life was the simple, straightforward process we'd like it to be, where everything worked according to plan, there would be no need for the kind of individuality we need to survive. However, life is not like that. It's always throwing up the unusual, the unique. In fact life's challenges occur precisely because things don't work out as planned. When we talk about coping with life's crises and challenges, we are talking about a set of problems that we all have to face as individuals and find our own way through; we can get general ideas about what worked in the past or what worked for other people in the past, but every individual has to find his or her own unique solution. This is why we don't learn from history and why you can't put an old head on young shoulders – nothing is ever the same twice.

We have to learn how to be different and how to be individuals because no rule, no law, no pattern of behaviour that we are taught can account for every occasion. If we learn to conform too much, we become powerless in the face of any

---

Whose law?

No theory about reality (be it Einstein's, your mother's or your father's) can be the reality it tries to describe. It always misses at some point precisely because it is a theory and because reality is a complex, ongoing flux of activity that presents itself differently to each individual. So there are always going to be conflicts between the theory and reality. As a child you have two parents who present in essence two different ideas about reality. These ideas overlap but they won't be exactly the same. If you've got brothers, sisters or friends, you'll get other ideas and see other ways of dealing with reality while also having your own ideas, your own wants and wishes that will help to shape your view of any situation.

new situation which doesn't obey the law or rule. We will never learn how to make our own rules, learn to think for ourselves, learn to cope with the unique events that make up our experience of life.

Rebellion and individuality

You can see that there is an element of rebellion involved in this process. At the same time as we are learning to be an individual, so too are we laying down the framework for the development of our ability to rebel. In fact they are two sides of the same coin. We rebel in order to be individuals.

The personality of our parents and the kind of relationship we have with them helps to dictate the nature of our own patterns of rebellion. This is a very easy concept to understand. We all have things we can get away with with our parents; there are some things we absolutely can't do, and some things we can do with one parent but not with the other and so on. Some parents will tolerate open differences of opinion and behaviour, others won't. Some are so controlling that their children dare not rebel at all in any way. Some children develop a kind of split life; behaving in one way with their parents and in a different way with other people.

All of us learn to develop various kinds of positive and negative patterns as part of our overall rebellious skills. They are a very important part of our personalities because as we grow up they evolve into a coping pattern that we bring to bear in any relationship from which we need something. They are the basis for how we later learn to express our upset and frustration with what we are getting from our relationships.

Confidence and coping

How you develop as an individual and how you rebel to a large extent determines how you cope with life's challenges. If your experience of rebelling and being different is pleasant, this immeasurably improves your ability to cope with challenges and problems. You feel confident and supported. You expect to cope with challenges.

This gives you a head start in learning coping skills because

Good and bad forms of rebelling

Good rebellions achieve something, they go somewhere and usually generate a mutual respect between the people involved. Healthy rebellions, like healthy arguments, make the participants think, expose flaws on both sides in a considerate way, open up avenues for new actions, thoughts and emotional exchanges, but above all result in a toleration of difference and individuality. Some people have very pleasant memories of rebellion; many creative people, for example, are creative precisely because their 'rebellions' were tolerated or encouraged.

Bad rebellions, like bad arguments, create running sores and inevitably achieve little beyond the realization that conflict exists. Usually there is little respect for individuality or difference, and rebellions are won or lost in terms of who can dominate at the time. The last thing that bad rebellions achieve is to make the participants think or to open up flaws and weaknesses for discussion. They leave you feeling unsatisfied and sometimes guilty. However, a bad rebellion is infinitely better than total submission. Sometimes you have to make do with a bad rebellion just to survive in a situation. As soon as you can, get out and find someone who will respect your differences and allow you to develop better rebellious skills.

one of the most important lessons in life we have to learn is how to deal with real challenges as opposed to dealing with personal differences and conflicts. If our parents take note of our rebellions and recognize that, yes, we do have a point and if they respond helpfully, then we don't get bogged down in futile acts of rebellion designed just to express distress and frustration. True coping skills tackle real issues and help you to find real solutions. If the opposite happens and your rebellions are condemned or lead nowhere, you get involved in simply trying to keep your emotional head above water. This makes it hard for you to move on and tackle reality; it's as if you get stuck on a treadmill of conflict.

You can see then that there are two senses in which we learn

Where there's a will, there's a way

Betty came from a difficult home. Her parents gave her
very little emotionally but spoilt her with gifts and money.
Betty rebelled from an early age and was a wilful and
spiteful child and teenager; it was the only way she could
get attention and be noticed. Later in adulthood she was
quite unable to cope with the demands of relationships,
or rather nobody could cope with her demands. Eventually
in middle-age and after two failed marriages she went to
a therapist for help. One of the first things she got Betty
to do was to re-examine her relationship with her parents
and so was able to show to her that how she had learnt
to survive in the face of two selfish parents had worked
then but now had to be unlearned. Betty had never progressed – she was still fighting with her parents and saw
every relationship in the same terms. Once she got an
insight into what was happening, Betty really got her act
together. She's still a difficult person but she has moved
on and has made a lot of new friends and is less wilful.

to cope. We learn to cope with the demands made on us by
our parents (and thus society) by learning to do fairly much
what they want us to do. And at the same time we learn to
cope in our own way with the gaps, weaknesses and blind
spots in the systems we are taught. You can see also that for
really successful survival we need to learn how to do both. If
we don't conform to what our parents want, we won't progress, won't fit in; we remain wilful, self-centred individuals.
If we don't learn to think for ourselves, we remain too dependent on our parents, too rule-bound and quite unable to look
after ourselves without our parents around. We remain
undeveloped as individuals.

Individuality and the outside world

Exposure to the outside world helps to strengthen the sense of
a child's place in the world in two ways. First it extends the

breadth and perspective of the value system the child has learned from its parents. Exposure to people in the outside world helps to deepen the child's sense of belonging to a community and, with this, they of course learn a wide range of fundamental social skills about how to fit into the community. Second, these interactions build on the pattern of coping and rebellion adopted by the child. They offer new avenues for rebellion, for example by joining in peer activities or by discovering intellectual, athletic or artistic interests that are encouraged by peers or teachers and which may not be encouraged at home. Peer group support can be enormously influential because it creates an alternative power and support system to that of the parents; it's a step on the way to forming your own intimate relationship and creating your own family. Essentially, it is peer group relationships that strengthen your sense of individuality largely through your contact with others who have similar problems and conflicts with building maps of reality. You learn that most people rebel in one way or another and that society allows for this to some extent by accepting individual differences.

Adolescence is a period of great change and challenge. While adolescents have to cope with the biological changes they are undergoing, they also have to develop a range of skills in preparation for entering the adult world. They learn for example the importance of being economically self-sufficient and they develop a wider view or map of what adult life is all about; they have to learn how to behave like an adult, to carry social responsibility and so on.

During this time adolescents also broaden their understanding of the complexity of life. For one thing, as they develop ties and attachments to their peers, so they start to explore new experiences in common with their friends; they experiment with relationships and friendships, in the process deepening their sexual and emotional contacts, and they explore the normal teenage mores of rebellion.

Adolescence offers a range of opportunities to learn skills and to develop relationships, but it also tests your ability to continue your development as an individual and to develop healthy coping patterns. While it can broaden your social and rebellious skills, it doesn't necessarily prepare you to cope with the real world any better as an individual. Part of being a teenager involves forming powerful relationships with your

What being an adult really means

Most teenagers eventually realize that societies are less than perfect entities, that there are problems, inconsistencies and injustices all around them. Just as they had to learn to make an adjustment to the gaps in the relationships they had with their parents, so they have to learn to live with the gaps between the ideology they have been fed about how society works and the reality of living in an imperfect society.

They learn about the various ways that adults cope with the gap between the theory of social promise and the reality. While some adults do rebel constructively and try to do something about the failings they see, many engage in what we can call the socially approved forms of rebellion that most societies have evolved to cope with frustration and conflict. Adult society offers a wide range of socially acceptable forms of escapism; for example we drink, smoke, eat and use medication to chase away our worries and frustrations, or we escape into voyeurism: we watch television, go to the cinema, sit in sports stadiums, play video games, and so on.

peers which help you to break your dependency on your parents, but this is often done by simply swapping one set of dependencies for another. While this is an important step on the long road to becoming a capable individual, it often involves having to conform excessively to the values and ideas of your peers. Although we all need to do this for some of the time, it is very easy to slip into this new conformity without retaining the ability to continue to think as an individual. You can for example end up rebelling for the sake of it and losing your individuality – and thus your ability to cope – in the crowd.

Adulthood

Theoretically, the onset of adulthood gives you the chance to develop fully your own place in the world as an individual.

Most of us spend our early years preparing to stand on our own feet, making use of the opportunities we have from our parents and peers to built up a strong base for setting out into life on our own. The social coping tasks we need to perform are quite clearly spelt out for us. By the time you're in your mid-twenties you are expected to be firmly on your own feet and be supporting yourself. Then gradually, especially after you get into a permanent relationship, you find yourself thinking of settling down, maybe starting a family, setting up home.

The coping tasks for the individual are less clearly spelt out. How we cope with the gaps between theory and reality both in society and within our private worlds is one of the big challenges we have to face during the transition from adolescence to adulthood. Faced with an often bewildering mass of options and ideas about life and living, each individual selects a mix of ideas and behaviours that seem easiest to live with or that best fit his or her own circumstances. Much of your adult life will be spent learning to make compromises as you cope with the ordinary challenges of being an adult and living in a society.

The tasks during this time are to learn to preserve your own personality, your own balance and sense of who you are in the face of the compromises you have to make. Those who cope well with challenges are those who have been able to keep this part of their functioning alive and well. While we all face similar challenges, we face them in unique situations – which means that we each have to find a solution that we can live with.

HEALTHY COPING

We are much closer now to being able to spell out what healthy coping means. As we've seen, the key to survival is the ability to learn the rules on the one hand but also to be able to break the rules sufficiently to become your own person, to be an individual when circumstances demand it. A key component of this process should be in place by the time you've finished with your adolescence – the ability to relate effectively with those around you. This survival skill has to be embedded in sets of relationships – with your parents, peers, friends – in order for it to work. It can't be done in isolation. What does this mean?

When things go wrong in your life, how do you cope? Well, one thing that helps you cope is if there is somewhere where you can feel safe, confident, loved, cared for and supported. We all tend to collapse in varying degrees when challenges come along, and it helps enormously if we have sufficiently strong relationships with those around us that allows for this. If you've been able to develop healthy relationships with your parents, they will always be there for you in this respect. Much the same is true of your relationships with your friends. If you don't have somewhere to go, it makes it harder to cope. You may feel isolated and alone to the extent that you may find the challenge overwhelming, get it out of proportion and cope badly.

What you need to cope successfully is a relationship, or a network of relationships, that allows you the space and time to be yourself, to be needy, to collapse, be cared for as a person, as an individual entity. A healthy relationship – be it with a parent or a friend – allows you to collapse a little without taking away your individuality. Unhealthy relationships are those which require you to be either too dependent or too independent, are one-sided, with no give and take, no reciprocity. Unhealthy coping is when you either do too much alone (coping alone) or need other people too much, and too much of the time.

One other point. To cope healthily requires that we are able to give expression to what we feel, especially in a crisis. We need room to give vent to our fears, tears, hopes and needs in a clear straightforward way. This is a matter of both biological and psychological health. Think of a frightened child running for comfort and security to its mother or father. Is there a more natural and healthy reaction? Then think of the parent brushing it off, pushing it away, stopping it crying, making it cope, grow up, or whatever actions the parent may choose to use, to stop the explosion of emotion. What this does to the child is unhealthy. You can apply the same logic to anyone, no matter what age, and yet so many people grow up under just this kind of learning condition, to the extent that sometimes they don't even realize what is happening to them. Some people lose touch completely with their emotions and use a variety of substitutes to express feelings to themselves and to other people. It goes without saying that part of healthy coping means that you can also give back to others close to you as much as they give to you.

Mother dear?

Janet's closest friend was her mother. Every time some-thing went wrong in Janet's life – a failed relationship, a lost job, a broken fingernail – she'd be on the phone to her mother. The trouble was that Janet hated having to do this. She always came away feeling shattered, and never changed, never learned to find other ways of coping. Why? Because while only her mother could give her the kind of attention she needed (her mother held her, fed her, let her cry), this attention lasted for half an hour. Then her mother would regale her with her own problems for hours thereafter in return for the half-hour of compas-sion. Her mother used Janet as she always had, as a kind of tame companion onto whom she could off-load her troubles. Janet always came away from these sessions exhausted and downhearted. Her mother never gave her enough and Janet lived in the hope that one day she would; but people of 79 rarely change.

When bad things happen to good relationships

Bob (52) and Lisa (48) had a miserable midlife period. Everything that could go wrong did. Bob lost his job and was unemployed for two years, one of their children had a bad accident and Lisa's father died. Plus Lisa had a tough menopause with a number of complications. But did they mind? Of course they minded, they hated it. But they had each established a good network of relationships beforehand and these served them well as each crisis came along. More importantly though, by the end of it all they had developed a much closer relationship with each other than they'd ever had before.

When midlife comes along, healthy copers will have usually built up a strong network of relationships that they feel com-fortable with. In times of change or crisis they are able to make use of these supportive relationships to help make them feel secure and cared for, but at the same time they are still able to think as individuals and are thus able to get a clear perspective on what the real issues and challenges are for them as people. They still think on their feet.

People who don't cope well end up feeling alone or isolated and have nowhere really they can turn. Janet, who we met above, had a terrible time of her menopause because, even though she had no hormonal problems to speak of, she had felt as if life was passing her by and the only person she could turn to treated her as a kind of emotional servant. Janet had spent so much time, invested so much in the relationship with her mother, that she'd not thought to use the time on more constructive relationships.

Being an adult can keep you busy; most of us get by. Those who get by better than average do so because they have good support systems and never lose sight of the fact that they are individuals.

Midlife with its changes tests your coping ability, as we have seen, but it also presents a major challenge to your sense of fulfilment and achievement as an individual. Midlife offers you, finally, the chance to put your life together, to make contact with the inner person that most of us lose touch with after adolescence and integrate it with who and what you are now. Although you are supposed to be a mature adult at 21, most of us only get the chance to develop and grow properly at midlife. Let me explain.

DREAM-MAPS

Part of the process of becoming an individual is that as we grow up and learn to cope with life, to fit in and find ourselves as people, so we gradually develop an idea of what we want for ourselves out of life. As we've seen, most of our childhood and adolescence is spent preparing to enter adult life in the sense of preparing to fit into society and take on adult responsibilities adequately. But an important part of our growing up is also spent in developing an expectancy that our hopes and dreams as individuals will also be fulfilled in our adult lives. Just as our physical and social development passes through stages, so too does this part of our existence.

Early dream-maps

As we saw earlier, there are areas of conflict in the growing child's relationship with his or her parents. The child learns through this conflict to develop a sense of individuality through rebelling and finding his or her own way of doing things. At the same time though the child also starts to construct a dream-map about how he or she ideally wants the world to be. How does this arise?

When a child's needs are cared for immediately there is no need for the child to think. Thinking usually starts when there is a delay, a gap if you like, between a need arising and the need being fulfilled. The hungry or uncomfortable child wants to be immediately cared for and if it is not, it starts to search for its parents or otherwise discover ways of getting its needs attended to. We begin the process of building a cognitive map of our world out of situations like this; we start making thought links between our needs and the whereabouts of our parents. We start to learn their habits and patterns. In short, we start to build a cognitive map of our world.

As the child gets older the map fills out gradually and the child learns that there can't be a perfect match between what it wants and what it gets. We recognize that we have to share things: we have to share Mum with Dad; we have to share time and goodies with other people like our siblings. But there is always a part of our thinking that wants it all, that yearns for some completely safe, holistic state in which we do have it all. This part becomes the dream or ideal map that we all develop. It is a fantasy construction, a dream fabric of bits of memories of good times and all the things we want, woven into an imagined perfect ideal of total satisfaction.

The essence of this early wish, or dream-map, nearly always involves ideal relationships. This is largely because it is people that fulfil our needs and are judged most likely to be able to give us satisfaction. In the early part of our childhood the dream-map focuses on our parents, but in time this is broadened to include other people as our contact with the outside world widens. What starts off in early childhood as a barely conscious fantasy map slowly becomes a major but relatively secret part of our thinking.

While we go around doing all the things that children do, an important part of our minds engages in dream-mapping. You may remember the kind of day-dreaming and fantasizing we all engaged in as youngsters; being a hero or heroine, being applauded, being famous, being brave, having wealth, and so on. These are ways we use to fantasize about having our dreams fulfilled, getting the attention or security we want. These dreams reflect also our desire to be something important in the world; the more flamboyant the dreams, the more we need to feel loved or worth something. You can see too how these dreams link to the kinds of careers that we will later choose; they are childlike versions of the kind of social goals painted for us by society.

Dreams, sex and emotions

The time between leaving childhood proper (at about six) and the onset of adolescence is a crucial one for the development of our dream-maps. As young children, there is a relatively close match between our ideal needs and what we actually get; parents usually provide for most of our needs and they give affection and attention fairly freely. For children in the older age group however, things are a bit different. We have to cope with the challenges of going to school and learning to deal with life outside the home. It can be a scary time and it is also the time when we most need our wishes, fears and anxieties attended to. It is also the time that a lot of the support we used to get as younger children is withdrawn. Overt affection is less freely given: for example, we are expected to behave more like grown-ups, to need less, to be more independent. The years between six and twelve can be something of an emotional desert as far as the practical fulfilment of these basic affectional needs is concerned, and you get a corresponding increase in dream-mapping or day-dreaming as the child struggles to cope. In fact the ability to dream is part of the coping process; when we are alone and struggling, it helps to be able to dream about being comforted and cared for. It gives us hope and helps us to carry on.

This unfulfilled wanting and yearning is expressed in our fantasy ideal map which is deeply personal and private – not shared, even with our closest friends lest we be considered childish or strange. At the same time we become more aware of the big outside world; we read or watch films, and the images we see help to flesh out our dream-maps, give us a sense of how our worlds could be if only we had the power to get what we want.

This process of dream-mapping is a subtle form of rebellion. You can tell by the fact that we feel ashamed of it, embarrassed by it – but we still do it. We dare not reveal that we need far more than we get, that we are often frightened and need comfort and support and affection. So instead we internalize it and fantasize about finding special people (and special relationships) who will do everything, give us everything that we want. This dream-map forms an important part of the rebellious pattern we each develop, and establishing a dream-map is intimately involved in the process of becoming an individual.

Two important events help to make this dream-map an integral part of our lives and less of a fantasy. Most of us can remember forming special, close relationships with significant people during this middle-childhood period; with a kind teacher, an older boy or girl or a friend. What marks these relationships off from other friendships is the intensity of feelings we have for them which can vie with the intensity of the feelings we have for our parents. We could call them crushes if you like, but they introduce us to the possibility of having our dreams fulfilled through a relationship. They may not be specific relationships; finding that you have a talent for something, say a sport or music, can give you the kind of reward and attention you need, and in the process help to give a grounding to your dreams.

Something else happens in this crucial time. We discover sex. Masturbation (and the fantasies that go with it) often begins in middle childhood, often well before the body is fully developed and long before the hormones for sexual development are fully active. Masturbation in a child is usually an expression of emotional need in response to the pressures of that age. It is also one of the first acts of personal rebellion we engage in; it's as if we have dared to give expression to our dream world. It's one of the first ways we have of developing our own sense of personal power – we learn to satisfy ourselves through our bodies. We can feel ashamed or guilty about this but like all forms of rebellion these acts are important steps on the road to individuality. They represent the first emotional steps we take away from our parents; we start the process of finding our satisfaction through other people and other things. They are a key link in the process of forming deeper contact with other people and we need them to cope with the challenges of adolescence.

Several crucial things happen to our dream-maps during adolescence. Perhaps the most important emerges from the deeper contact we have with our peers usually in the form of shared sexual, spiritual or affectional experiences. There are many forms this contact can take. Shared religious experience is one; lots of teenagers go through quite intense religious experiences (or perhaps we could call them philosophical experiences because they could be of a political, ideological or ecological nature). Music and dance are other ways that dream-mapping is shared. I'm not necessarily talking about the social forms these take whereby to be a teenager you have to like certain approved music or dance forms, but rather those experiences where you share a moment of musical or dance ecstasy with someone that moves you beyond the simple pleasure of dancing or listening to music.

These shared experiences tap into our dream-maps; the fact that others can share these feelings and can talk or do something about them encourages us to believe that our dreams can come true. Falling in love, though, has an even bigger impact. When you fall in love as a teenager it taps into your dream-map in a very powerful way, which is why teenage love is such an intense experience. Most teenagers fall in love cerebrally at first; you might have a crush on a teacher, a friend, a pop or movie star. This is essentially a fairly simple extension of dream-mapping and you don't feel too bad about it because most of your friends are doing it too and because society also encourages it. When it gets physical, though, when touch and sex enter into the picture as well, things change. This is partly because physical contact brings new experiences of great intensity and partly because it opens up a whole range of anxieties about yourself and your behaviour which you have previously managed to contain. It becomes personal, between you and the other person; you're on your own, no longer just part of a crowd.

When you fall in love, you trust that the other person's dream-map is the same as yours. You've always kept your dream-map a secret. Now you start to share it. You make your secret rebellion more open. You might find yourself talking about yourself and your home life in ways you've never done before: you might criticize your parents for example and talk about things that worry you. You'll show affection and do sexual things. You may feel terribly guilty and anxious about all these developments, partly because you feel you're betraying your parents in some way, partly because you'll be afraid of the consequences of exposing your dream-needs.

Adolescent anxiety is a massive thing. You feel strange anyway; you're growing and changing: you're half-child, half-adult. You feel a mixture of self-consciousness and excitement. You're unsure. Your relationships are changing, even your relationship with your parents. It's a mess, and you're scared. A great deal of your confidence depends on your ability to translate your dream-map into reality, but all you've got to go on is your experience of being a child and being relatively powerless. As we've seen, the dream-map part of you has evolved as a means of coping with the gaps and holes in reality that you've seen in the past. In some ways it has helped you hold yourself together, given you hope for the future. In adolescence when you are in love, the future is now.

Just as important as falling in love is the experience of falling out of love. Sometimes the experience can be shattering. Once you've taken the step of trusting another person with these very intimate parts of yourself, you can feel very vulnerable and exposed. You need to be loved and to love. When your first really deep love affair breaks up, you feel as if you're going to die emotionally, and how you cope with this can make a great deal of difference to you in the future.

Some teenagers never really recover from this episode; they never again trust in the same way, and they stop working on their dream-maps. They may continue to dream but they keep it inside themselves. They may relate again, grow up, marry, have children, but they never again want to share this part of themselves. We mustn't forget how important this is; suicide is one of the major causes of death during adolescence largely because of this kind of collapse of relationship. The collapse of relationships is also one of the greatest sources of adult unhappiness.

Other teenagers, unable to cope with the sense of devastation and loss of their first opening-up experience, launch themselves into fresh relationships of one kind or another. Some people become wary of trusting only one person and may become promiscuous. Others go through a lengthy series of relationships, each collapsing at key points in the process of learning to share dreams.

Most teenagers make a compromise: that is, they are able to make relationships but they always retain a part of themselves, a part of their dream-mapping that they don't share with others even if they want to. Some people can lead quite split lives, sharing parts of themselves with some people and different parts with other people. Some people pour their energy into other areas. Perhaps dissatisfied with their early relationships, they react by throwing themselves into finding other ways of filling the gaps in their dream-maps. You can see this for example in the way people throw themselves into their careers or into making money or into some other activity that helps them to feel that their dream-needs are being satisfied.

Adult dreams

The dream-maps we develop give a direction to our individuality. Each stage of life offers fresh opportunities to work on our dream-maps, and none more so than adult life when there is more opportunity to become an individual. Despite the disappointments and gaps of childhood and adolescence, most of us enter the adult world full of optimism that somewhere along the way we will get our dreams fulfilled. Of course we are helped in this by the promises that our society has taught us to hold out for; that is, that we will be happy in our chosen career role, find the right person to fall in love with, find happiness and fulfilment in a relationship, in marriage, in having children, and so on. Most of us are brought up to believe in these myths. Even if we rebel against the social form that these myths take, as the Woodstock generation did, at heart – especially in our dream-mapping hearts – we still believe that our dreams will come true.

Becoming an adult and becoming an individual are not necessarily the same thing. As we have seen, each developmental stage – childhood, adolescence and adulthood – presents two tasks for a person to master: to learn how to cope with the social expectations that society demands as a condition for fitting in, and to maintain a sense of individuality, to achieve an idea of our own worth, including – as we now can see – the fulfilment of some of our more important dreams.

Most people manage to some extent to achieve the former; they learn to stand on their own feet, they form relationships, follow careers, and so on. They look like adults; they do adult things. But are they individuals?

As society is constituted at the moment, the answer is No. During adulthood as we define it these days, there is very little time to be an individual or to work at our dream-maps. Some people of course do achieve their dreams during adulthood and become individuals in the fullest sense of that word; for a variety of reasons they have the opportunity to act on their dream-plans and they have the opportunity to be themselves. We all know of people (inevitably more dynamic than most) who try to fulfil their dream-plans. But for many people this is not the case. They remain bogged down by their circumstances, their social roles, their conventional forms of rebellion, waiting for something to happen to change their circumstances. This is one of the reasons why so many people believe in chance or luck or some other external force; they have no faith or belief in their own ability to make changes.

In a sense life has – at least for most people – always been like this. It has only been in recent years that people have begun to realize that there is in fact more to life than simply coping with conventional social pressures, and that finding yourself as an individual is not just the domain of the wealthy or the successful. As we saw earlier, midlifers of today are the first generation to have experienced the extra longevity and benefits that contemporary society has to offer. They have been in the forefront of challenging the validity of social prescriptions.

Most people do not have the resources to make things change for themselves. Most of us go with the flow of social demands and pressures. Much of your status and most of your actions are dictated by the roles you have to play as a provider, a wife, a mother, a husband, a father. There is little social recognition of your dream-needs, and so you continue as perhaps you always have, getting some dream-satisfaction through relationships, books, films, day-dreams or fantasies. Most of us reach midlife with large parts of our individual needs contained in our dream-maps untouched and undeveloped; thoughts we never expressed, actions we never took, love we didn't give, love we didn't receive.

For most people the only thing that can happen to change their circumstances is for something outside themselves to modify the pressures they are under. Some people experience changed circumstances early on in their adulthood – the death of a spouse, unemployment or other economic crises – or they may inherit money or otherwise improve their circumstances. For the vast majority of people in our society, the onset of the events that we call midlife is the first time since adolescence that something changes in their lives and they get the opportunity to look again at their individual needs and their dream-maps.

INDIVIDUALITY: THE GREAT CHALLENGE OF MIDLIFE

Midlife offers the last opportunity we have in life to develop as individuals precisely because things change during this period. Every one of the changes that come up during midlife creates the opportunity to focus on the challenge of becoming your own person and making something real out of your dream-map:

1 *Ageing*
   As a child, as an adolescent, and as a young adult, we don't much think about time – we're young, life stretches out ahead of us. Time is what we have plenty of; midlife forces us into having to think about what we're going to do in the time we have left. Age changes also force us to reappraise some of our values; if for example you've traded on your looks, wrinkles and sagging skin can seriously affect your view of yourself. Fear of ageing is really a fear of running out of time before you can get to know yourself or before your dreams can become reality.

2 *Biological changes*
   Midlife brings you back to your biological nature and raises questions about how you feel about your body, how you've used and abused it, and above all what you are going to do about it in order to get the most out of it in the future. Midlife biological problems like the menopause or becoming impotent can upset your equilibrium as an individual, forcing you – perhaps for the first time in life – to seek help or comfort. One of the important but little-appreciated conse-

quences of becoming an individual is that it can help you survive in old age when those around you pass on. Look at some older couples: they appear to be clinging to each other for safety – little wonder that when one goes, the other follows soon after. If only they had realized in their midlife years that things they could have done then could have radically changed their experience of old age.

3 *Changes in relationships*
Midlife can bring with it changes in many of your basic relationships; with your partner, your children, your parents, friends and colleagues. These changes may disrupt your sense of personal security, raise doubts about who you are as an individual, and raise questions about what you want from your relationships. You get the chance to find out what your relationships really mean and who you really are.

4 *Changes in the family*
Watching your children growing into adolescents, dealing with, teaching or working with younger people in general can make you feel old and make you wonder what you're going to do now that you may no longer be needed in the same way as in the past.
   Coping with an adolescent in the family or with other young people can be one of the most challenging experiences a middle-aged person has to face, and it can hit you in ways no other experience can. They often challenge and question your authority, values and personality in ways that no one else can. Watching younger people grow up can remind you of yourself at the same stage. You see in what they are going through some of the pain and excitement you experienced when you were their age, and this can revive some of your long-dormant interest in your own dream-mapping. You may begin to wonder about yourself, your relationships and where you're going. Having to deal with your ageing parents may give you an insight into where you may be going if you don't do something about yourself.

5 *Changes in obligations*
We spend our childhood and adolescence preparing to cope with adult life and its demands. We spend our adult life surviving, looking after other people, fulfilling our obli-

gations. At midlife, our time has come, we've paid our dues, our obligations are by and large behind us: now it's time for us. If you have children and they leave home, this can help to make realization of this fact a concrete reality in that it may give you the emotional and physical time to think.

6 *Career changes*
Career pressures can change at midlife. You may want to re-think how you earn your income, or want to try something new. With your obligations reduced, you have the opportunity to do something that better suits your personality or fulfils an old dream – or even a new dream.

Midlife's great challenge is to see these events for what they really are – the opportunity to become yourself. Now it's time to fulfil your personal responsibility to yourself as *an individual*, to look again at that secret dreaming part of yourself and give it the opportunity to develop and grow, to look again at how you have coped in the past, how you have expressed your rebellious self. Above all, midlife is about re-examining the compromises you have made in your life, with yourself, with your body, in your relationships, in your career and with your family.

| THE KEY ISSUE | *Moving forward* |

In the past there were few guide-lines to help people cope with this challenge of becoming individuals and most people had to get by as best they could. The issue is how to tackle the challenge, how to act constructively and usefully.

The person entering midlife now has a much broader range of options for rebellion than did previous generations. It is much easier today to change your relationships or how you relate; there is much greater tolerance for individuality and it has become acceptable to explore yourself and your needs through sexual and relational experimentation, through touch, massage, spiritual fulfilment, and so on. The present midlife generation is used to searching and used to rebelling.

The problem is that while things seem to have improved, it

is far too easy to get involved in acts of apparent searching and rebellion that do not actually deal with the real issues that people need to face during midlife. We are experts in our society at getting involved in things that take our minds off ourselves and our problems; we are great escapists. Just as medication or rejuvenation programmes – the more conventional forms of coping with midlife changes – can help to take our minds off things and give us hope and temporary relief, so can adopting a conventional form of rebellion. Both leave you no further along the path of exploring yourself. Having an affair, for example, may do wonders for your ego and lift you out of a midlife depression, but it can also be a powerful thought-blocker distracting you from dealing with the underlying issues contained in your own personality and individual circumstances.

The difficulty is that coping with the challenge of midlife is not something that can be prescribed for you. Dream-mapping is a personal, individual matter. The thing about the challenge of becoming an individual during midlife is that it is precisely that – becoming an individual, finding your own way. This time, though, the task is to rebel for yourself and by yourself. This time it is not a case of learning to rebel against your parents as you did as a child or to rebel against society as you did as an adolescent. Now it is a matter of rebelling against the life you have constructed for yourself and against the choices and compromises you have made for yourself. You have to re-define your own reality.

What I've tried to show in this chapter is the importance of the concept of becoming an individual. I've also tried to show how important rebellion is, that it helps us to achieve levels of contact and a sense of individuality that we can't get through simply conforming to the *status quo*. It is so important to recognize that there are significant tasks for the individual to confront in midlife, because how you deal with midlife challenges will help you cope with what happens when you enter old age. When you get into old age there is still a lot of emotional work to do. For one thing you have to face up to your own end, to the fact that you are going to die. For another, you have to re-work some of your relationship with your children who by then will themselves be in midlife. But this is the subject of another book.

I mention it here because a great deal depends on how you

manage the opportunity you have in midlife to take up the challenges you face. At midlife you have to start thinking for yourself, you have to look at how you've been living and hopefully make changes that will help you to survive healthily. Only then, I believe, will you be in a good position to take on the challenges of old age. What you decide to do now about your health for example will help determine whether or not you actually live long enough to reach old age. Similarly, what you decide to do now about your relationships will help shape the kind of circumstances that you'll be facing if and when you get *really* old.

What I'm going to do in the rest of the book is to spell out the areas that need working on if you want to discover yourself as a person. In the process I hope that you'll begin to see just what is involved in becoming a real-life rebel, see what the real challenges are. I want to look at four main areas – the challenges posed by personal relationships, those inherent in family relationships, and in career challenges, and lastly the health challenges that you will sooner or later have to face.

CHAPTER FIVE

Try a Little Intimacy

I can remember at 17 buying a couple of books on psychology and relationships in my attempt to come to terms with my own adolescent struggles, and they were a great help because they broadened my understanding of how other people related and the kind of problems they had. But my friends teased me for thinking that I could get information like that out of a book, so I was a bit secretive about it. Mind you, my male friends were always grilling me about what the books actually said, and my female friends would often refer me to articles they'd read in women's magazines, so I think there was a common need there somewhere.

We are taught very little about relationships as we grow, and most of us only seek out information when things go wrong or if we have trouble getting what we want out of our existing relationships. Society educates us through a series of interlocked relationships; our relationships with our parents, with our siblings and friends and teachers. We learn through this set of relationships how to think about relating and what relating means, and much of what we imbibe is accepted unquestioningly and unthinkingly. It's not like the formal learning we get at school or the techniques we acquire when we learn a skill; it is tacit, informal learning. We adopt attitudes, opinions, beliefs and ways of behaving through these relationships, and they affect the way we think, the things we say, the way we talk, the way we dress and express ourselves. Most importantly, we learn a social identity through our relationships: we learn about who or what we are in a social sense. Finally, we are supposed to end up, as young adults, by getting involved in our own intimate relationship with someone else, have children and start the whole process all over again.

Apart from the social function that intimate relationships serve they also serve a vital personal function. Throughout our lives these relationships provide us with a sense of our own personal worth and serve as a source of security. As young children we get our security and sense of well-being almost entirely from the personal relationships we form with our parents, and as we grow up through adolescence and adulthood we transfer these needs to the other relationships we form. We bring therefore to our intimate relationships a full set of our past baggage, our needs and our coping patterns.

Being in an intimate relationship is perhaps the most challenging situation we can ever find ourselves in. Many of the relationships we form as we find our place in the world can be challenging; you can struggle making friends, for example, or you may find relationships at work a challenge, but none of these taps you as fully as an intimate relationship does. You have to learn to share your personal space with someone else in a way that you have never done before; you have to share your body, your sleeping space, your toilet habits, your rest and relaxation habits, and so on. Intimate relationships can also challenge your ability to believe in yourself and to protect yourself; relationships can sometimes turn into a battle of wills or a power struggle between the partners. This can test how well we cope when we don't get what we want, show up how we rebel and how we express anger and frustration.

We also come to our relationships with sets of ideas and expectancies about what we want out of them for ourselves. We all have tucked away somewhere a dream-map that we hope we will be able to share with our partners; relating is the arena in which we expose some of the most vulnerable parts of our personalities to another person. These can be romantic or deeply-felt ideas about relating, but they can also be more pragmatic. Some people get into relationships for security, out of a fear of being alone, out of a need to belong somewhere. Some get into relationships to please their parents and friends, some to rebel against their families, some to escape from troubled home lives. These may have served their purpose at the time but may need reviewing at midlife because circumstances may have changed.

The difficulty is that much of what we learn about how to

conduct our intimate relationships doesn't necessarily teach us all that much about what is actually involved in being in a relationship. And this can make it very hard to re-assess our relationships and our compromises at midlife. A great deal of what we learn about relationships is the social form that relationships are expected to take; how they should be structured, what they should look like, what each partner's roles should be and so on. Don't forget that our intimate relationships serve an important social function. Society uses them as its basic social and economic unit: we live as couples, earn money and raise our children in the units we call the nuclear family. Practically all that we are taught focuses on how to make our intimate relationships best serve these functions. We learn what relationships are for society; what we don't learn is what relationships could be for us as individuals. This framework seems to work so long as the social ends are being served, but what happens when those social functions are fulfilled?

RELATIONSHIPS AT MIDLIFE

This is precisely what happens during the midlife period. At some point during midlife, you reach the end of your parenting period, of your child-rearing responsibilities, and suddenly you're faced with the full complexity of dealing with an intimate relationship. Suddenly, at midlife, some of the glue that holds relationships together comes unstuck. With the children gone or about to go, with a degree of economic security attained, with some career goals perhaps achieved, there is a lessening of pressure. There's time to look again at a relationship that may well be based on a set of compromises made 20 years earlier under entirely different circumstances.

There are few opportunities in life to explore ourselves fully as individuals and to try to work out our dreams; midlife changes offer a fresh opportunity to do these things. And quite apart from other roles that our intimate relationships may play, they provide an arena for exploration of intimacy like no other; they are one of the last frontiers of uncharted territory left for us to explore – getting to know ourselves and those close to us.

Our relationships also play a major role in helping to shape how we cope with the challenges of midlife because they can help or hinder the process of finding ourselves as individuals.

Practically everything that we have to do for ourselves at
midlife will have an effect on our intimate relationships and
vice versa. If you want to change your career or develop a new
one, find new ways of spending your time, or just change your
health habits, a great deal depends on those around you and
how they react. Their approval can encourage you; their dis-
approval can sink your every effort.

The basic challenge that middle-aged people face in their
relationships is to take a long, hard look at the kind of compromises they have made, to re-examine the basis on which
the compromises were made, and where possible to renegotiate
new levels and patterns of relating. This is a broad statement,
I know, and some people won't need to do this simply because
they may perhaps always have done it, but many people reach
midlife desperately in need of such a re-evaluation of their lives
and their relationships.

Some people may be trapped in an unhappy relationship,
afraid to do something about it. Society presents a picture of
ideal relating: a perfect partnership with love conquering all. If
it doesn't work, it preaches tolerance, patience and encourages
the belief that it will all come right. Somewhere in the background is the suggestion that if it doesn't go right you are somehow inadequate or unlovable. Worse, if you do have problems
or want to change things, you're made to feel bad or guilty –
as if you don't fit in, as if there's something wrong with you,
that you've failed as an individual. This is a great pressure and
one of the reasons why people so often stay in relationships
even when they are lonely and unhappy, dissatisfied and frustrated.

Some people may be in relationships that have worked up to
a point, perhaps when there were children to raise or careers to
be built, but which seem empty or unfulfilling at midlife. When
we are young we all learn the words for what relating involves.
We talk about love and trust, closeness and caring, and there is
a great deal of social and personal glue around to ensure that
at least initially the words and the reality seem to match. In the
beginning for example much of the momentum of being loved
and loving another carries you through. Moreover, just having
a relationship or being married brings us a certain status in
society and the same goes for having children; both help to
cement the notion that dreams can come true. The difficulty is
that these early experiences are only part of the picture; many

A classic dilemma

Maureen had married Garth, her boss, when he was in the aftermath of a nasty divorce. The relationship worked for a long time, nearly 20 years. But as time passed by Maureen began to feel that they were not sexually or emotionally compatible, that things just had not turned out the way she had dreamt they would. Garth found it hard to keep up with Maureen, who had blossomed out in the relationship and had slowly become more adventurous and outgoing.

The initial conditions in which the relationship had started no longer existed. Garth had married his secretary and for him the relationship had been ideal; he'd wanted someone to care for him and let him be the boss. Maureen was happy to do this at the time, but her needs had changed while his had not. Marriage to her boss had given her confidence and taken care of deep-seated anxiety about herself; she'd always wanted to be married to someone who could protect her and had never really thought beyond this. Freed of this anxiety, she had begun to explore her own sexual and emotional needs for the first time in her life and she soon found that at this level Garth was only interested in his needs not hers. It had not mattered in the past but now it did; she realized that she'd been attracted by Garth's power and not to him as a person. They couldn't talk to one another, couldn't find a way through. At the same time they couldn't leave one another because both were afraid of the consequences; Garth felt he was too old to start again and Maureen was afraid to give up the security she felt with Garth. What they needed to do was change the base of their relationship: keep what was good in it, acknowledge the limitations and allow each other the freedom to explore themselves responsibly as individuals. This was a tough option they simply were not prepared to take; instead they have slowly been destroying each other with their anger and hurt.

people get into relationships early on for reasons that may have little to do with tapping into their deeper needs for a relationship. As they age, their emotional needs change and what was once considered to be a satisfying relationship can seem eventually like a millstone around the neck. You grow up expecting that your intimate relationship will provide for all your needs. When or if it doesn't, you're faced with the challenge of what to do about it.

Other people may have no relationship worth talking about and feel miserable about it. They may have tried and failed or never tried at all. They may have to re-examine how they form relationships, try to work out where things go wrong or even whether or not they really want or need a relationship.

Examining your compromises

When we re-examine our relationships we need to consider three basic issues. We have to look at the choices we made and see in what ways social pressures may have helped us to make these choices. We need to look at those pressures to see if they still obtain and if they can be modified or changed. Secondly we need to look at the nature of our partners and see if there

---

Is life trying to tell you something?

Bev could not exist without a relationship. She had to have a man around. At 51, after three divorces and countless failed relationships, she had finally to recognize that something, somewhere was wrong. Yet she was still convinced that what was wrong was simply that she had just not met Mr Wonderful. What was really wrong was that Bev had never faced up to her fear of being on her own, of caring for herself, exploring herself. When she did – after a lot of soul-searching – she realized that perhaps after all she preferred her own company most of the time. Sometimes it's a matter of getting to know yourself better first rather than trying to get everything you want for yourself from another person or relationship.

is room for making changes with them; we also need to find out in what ways we may be hindered by our partners in achieving what we want. Lastly we need to look closely at ourselves and see in what ways we ourselves are hindering our own development.

Having said that, though, bear in mind that when we talk about impediments to re-examining our relationships it is important that we don't see our problems as being solely caused by society, our partners or ourselves. It is more complicated than that. We have to take care for example to differentiate between saying that society or our partners can *hinder* the development of proper intimacy and saying that society or our partners *cause* problems in relationships. It's all very well blaming society or your partner for your problems but neither society nor your partner necessarily forces you to conform with what they want. A great deal depends on whether or not you've learnt to develop your own ability to rebel constructively against the rules you've been brought up with in the sense we discussed in the last chapter.

Is younger better?

Ever wondered why so many middle-aged men and, increasingly, women go after young, glamorous people? Part of the reason is because they are chasing a dream or fantasy that has remained in their minds unworked since they were themselves young. Often these people think of themselves (in their inner selves) as being young even if they're pushing 50. They're right. Parts of their emotional needs are young and need developing. If you don't explore your dreaming, share it with people and work on it, it doesn't grow, it stays stuck at the level at which you did explore it, which is usually in adolescence and early adulthood.

Another reason is because some middle-aged people feel safer, more in control, relating to younger people; they use their greater age and experience to achieve a position of power they didn't feel they possessed when relating to someone of their own generation.

Examining your compromises requires care and thought. It isn't easy to reflect without getting lost in the process of attributing blame. We are not encouraged to reflect properly on the ideal social model; if a relationship fails, someone, according to society, has to be blamed, and few people are taught how to reflect constructively on their lives. This is one of the reasons why people sometimes rebel impulsively; they feel things are not right, find someone to blame and then go off at half-cock only to regret their actions later amidst a mass of guilt and recrimination – which is precisely what happened to Mark.

Mark, married for 18 years with two children, suddenly had a midlife crisis at the age of 54 during which he turned his life upside down. He met a much younger woman, fell for her in a big way, and decided to leave his wife and family without a word of warning. His wife woke up one Monday morning to find he'd packed and gone and simply left a note on the kitchen table announcing his decision.

'I'd always been torn inside. On the one hand I was quite happy with Ellen and of course I loved the family and everything. But in a sense I was always living somewhere else in my head. I never felt that I was happy sexually, there was always a part of me that was on the watch for the woman of my dreams. I used to look at how other men lived and really envied them their freedom, you know, to do what they wanted, to live life as they wanted. In contrast my life was so organized and conventional. I used to wish I could meet someone who could take me away from all this conformity but I never had the courage to do anything drastic. I was too scared to leave Ellen and the family. I was like an accident waiting to happen. Then I met Linda – she was so different from Ellen, sexy in a way Ellen could never be. I thought about it; the kids were through high school, I wasn't getting any younger, so I decided to go for it. I feel terribly guilty about it but I took my chance. Linda is everything I want.'

Mark's case is something of a classic; he had married Ellen for all the good social reasons, but like many people he had a secret dream-map that he was obsessed by and which he'd never shared or worked on. He spent a lot of time and poured a lot of energy into fantasizing about finding an ideal woman. When I asked him whether or not he had ever tried to talk about his needs to Ellen or anyone else, or to do something about his needs himself, he was surprised at the question; he'd not thought that maybe some of the problem lay inside himself and how he had dealt with his fantasy needs.

The point about Mark was that while he was right to do something about his frustrations, what he did and how he conceived of his problems was impulsive and thoughtless. He took a gamble that in changing women he would get lucky. Some people are lucky and manage to make a better match the second or third time round, but it really is often just a matter of luck. Mark unfortunately didn't have luck; Linda stayed with him for just over a year, got tired of being his fantasy figure, and then decided to leave him for another man. Mark was devastated – he'd truly thought that Linda had felt exactly the same about him as he had about her. So finally he was left with having to get down to the task of taking a long, hard look at himself.

Part of the problem in cases such as these lies in the way people think about getting their dreams fulfilled, and part of the problem lies in the way society teaches us to think about relationships. If you've brought people up to believe that somewhere outside there is a Mr or Ms Right waiting for them and if you don't encourage them to think about relationships very deeply, it makes it very easy for a frustrated person to think that the solution lies in simply changing partner. If this happens during midlife it's easy to dismiss it as simply a midlife crisis, which helps to obscure what is really going on and what needs to be done.

Many people react to midlife relationship problems too quickly and too simplistically. They make radical changes not only because society trains them to look for simple solutions but also because acting quickly and impulsively helps them to avoid facing any guilt and anxiety they may feel. And this is the point: re-examining your compromises requires careful thought and analysis. It takes time and some soul-searching because far more is involved than most people realize.

Let me give you an idea of what I mean. Wendy is a good example of someone who was confronted by all three of the impediments mentioned above in her attempt to find herself during midlife. At 45 she was locked into a marriage with three children and a husband who was totally wrapped up in his career. She was unhappy, dissatisfied with her relationship and with herself. She felt old, unattractive and unfulfilled. She'd met and married her husband when she was 23, and

Fantasies

These tell us a great deal about ourselves, and in Mark's case they showed that apart from his social life he wanted some excitement and stimulation to balance his otherwise mundane existence. In ditching his one life for another he was looking for someone to make it all happen for him. He changed nothing fundamentally because he didn't realize that we have to make our dreams and fantasies come alive for and by ourselves. Mark was essentially an unassertive and shy person, waiting for other people to make his life interesting. His fantasies showed that there was another side to him just waiting to get out. Like the fantasies of many such men, these focused on having some amazing woman coming along to pull his own passion out of him.

What Mark could have tried was making his life exciting for himself by trying new things, sharing his feelings with his wife and exploring her needs and fantasies as well as his own. Part of growing up at midlife involves taking responsibility for our inner dreams and finding out what they mean about us and our partners. When Mark did get to work on himself, he became a different person, more assertive, more sensitive to others, and his fantasies became more realistic. Encapsulated, back-of-your-mind fantasies remain masturbatory aids. Worked-out fantasies are achievable because the act of working through them creates real emotional tasks for us to sort out in the real world.

---

they had got on well for the first six or seven years as they busied themselves doing all the socially relevant things. They'd also done their share of rebelling as youngsters, taken part in the 1960s revolutions and considered themselves a modern, sophisticated couple, but over the past five years they'd slowly grown apart.

Wendy was very close to her parents and they had always played a major role in her life and in her thinking. She'd married the kind of man her parents liked, and lived the kind of life they approved of, and although she was desperately unhappy with the way things had gone she had never said a word to them about it. In fact until she was 40 she hadn't even talked to her best friends about her problems. She'd certainly never thought of doing anything overt about it because, as she said, she would feel too guilty, feel disloyal. Eventually she had confided in her friends, one or two who were in similar predicaments, and used this contact to express her rebellious ideas and frustrations. Encouraged by her friends, she'd had a brief affair which had caused her to feel a great deal of guilt. When I saw her, her main focus of concern was on dealing with this guilt – so much so that she'd had no time to think through things properly.

Underneath the guilt Wendy was angry. Angry with men, particularly with her husband for the way he neglected her and always put his career first, angry with society for not recognizing her dilemma, and angry with herself for lacking the courage to do something more constructive about her situation.

Wendy's problems were quite deep-rooted; she had never rebelled for herself in her life; she was her parents' blue-eyed daughter and was greatly admired by them for her marriage and conduct, and for being a good mother. This was in contrast to her elder brother and sister who had been rebellious and were regarded as the black sheep of the family. Wendy was a product of parents who did not allow their children to develop their own rebellious skills and find their own way of doing things with confidence. She always did what she was told and what was expected of her, whether by society, her parents or her husband.

Wendy did rebel when she was cross or upset, but in the subtle and passive ways she'd learnt at home; she would get a headache for example, or sulk and withdraw. She would never be outspoken or confrontational, and she had never learnt to develop her own assertiveness. The problem was made worse by the fact that the only time she had rebelled in her life, by having an affair, left her feeling worse than she'd ever felt. Because Wendy hadn't learnt to rebel, and had no confidence in her ability to do so, she was constantly being torn between opposing arguments she had with herself. Instead of doing anything about it she'd waste hours alternating between trying to justify her anger on the one hand, and feeling guilty for being angry on the other. So she was in a sense her own worst enemy, and the situation was further hindered by the fact that she had an uncommunicative and defensive husband and two overbearing and over-protective parents.

Wendy needed to learn how to rebel and gain confidence in her ability to get her own needs attended to; she needed to learn how to express her anger and frustration more constructively and not take it out on herself through guilt and headaches. If you haven't learnt to rebel and think for yourself, life in an intimate relationship can be terribly frustrating. You end up doubting your right to your own needs, and you spend your time trying to conform to patterns of relating that are out of place in a proper intimate relationship. Much of what we are taught is gender-based, and this was one of the things that Wendy was struggling with because it had been heavily reinforced by her parents and by her husband.

Gender differences in our society probably account for many of the problems experienced by couples in relationships, and they can become particularly pronounced during midlife when you are trying to rethink who you are. Gender training applies to a wide range of behaviours; you're taught to express (or not to express) emotions, thoughts, values and attitudes according to what society thinks is appropriate for your gender. Little boys very soon learn for example that there is a great embargo on the expression of the so-called feminine emotions like crying, sensuality, gentleness and delicacy, and at the same time great approval for the so-called masculine traits of toughness, power and control.

Little girls experience something very similar. They are discouraged from developing masculine traits and have to be very careful how they express emotions such as anger and other robust feelings. At the same time they are encouraged to concentrate on their softer sides and on the social roles society accords women: looking good, being feminine, being maternal, and so on. It is hard to unlearn these roles as you sometimes have to in close relationships, and it's even harder to go against these prescriptions if you have never been taught how to rebel.

What Wendy was struggling with was the parts of her that didn't fit into these patterns. She needed to find avenues to express herself without worrying about whether she'd be thought strange or unfeminine. Like all people she was a great deal more complex than could be described by the social stereotypes she'd learnt to impose on herself. Fortunately Wendy was eager to explore herself and her relationship, and slowly over time, with help, she learnt to tackle the fear she felt about being assertive and was able to achieve a much better balance

---

Wendy's action list

This list contains some good advice for people trying to find themselves.

1 Do things for yourself, not always for others; for instance in the way you wear your clothes or hold opinions; or take trips, get fit, and so forth.
2 Get used to being anxious about asserting yourself in such a way. This anxiety will help to drive your thinking. In time it will go away.
3 Don't use old ways of coping with your anxiety – no more excuses, no headaches, no binges, no silent anger.
4 Instead articulate your feelings; have conversations with yourself to reassure yourself of your rights. Show emotion.
5 When you're used to doing this alone, try it out on people you feel safe with, and then do it with the people who are making you anxious.
6 Stay calm and don't get fraught. Learn to use anger constructively and appropriately – for instance when you are insulted or overridden – and do something about it. Don't be afraid to walk away from arguments or put-downs if they get out of hand.
7 Open your eyes to your effect on other people. Learn to get a sense of your own power and how you may be influencing situations both negatively and positively.
8 Develop your real skills. Get a sense of humour, explore yourself.
9 Plan and think for yourself; nobody else will. Stop waiting for someone else to fix things or for things to change.

---

in her life. She read books, talked to people and gradually became much more confident about her own rights. It was quite startling to discover to what extent she had given in to the pressures she was under; one of her first acts of rebellion was to choose her own clothes and risk her mother's condemnation. Wendy had always chosen clothes of which she knew her mother would approve. After a while Wendy was able to tackle her husband, and together they hammered out a mode of co-existence that seemed to satisfy them both. It wasn't perfect, but Wendy at last was on the road to self-discovery; she took on new tasks and her career really blossomed. Her husband though was lost; he didn't know how to manage the new Wendy and in time he had to get his own act together.

Wendy is a good example of someone who had many impediments to finding out about herself and re-examining her relationship. But at least she'd got further in her examination than many: some dare not even think about their relationships let alone contemplate change.

All of us are under tremendous social personal pressure to maintain the *status quo* in our relationships, and this can make it very hard to think and act constructively. Many of us are capable of being critical of society yet can find it hard to question our partners and our relationships. One difficulty is that our relationships can be a source of great security. Sometimes too much so; the thought of change can create great tension and distress. It's easy to hide behind the security of our relationships and to forget that they develop as a set of compromises made between two individuals, and that these two individuals grow and change as they age.

How your partner reacts to your attempts to do things for yourself and your attempts to re-examine your compromises

---

A worst-case scenario

Magda's husband takes little notice of her, does much as he likes – including having affairs – and has somehow managed to make Magda feel it's all her fault. He's a charming, gregarious, good-looking chap in a superficial, social way, and most of Magda's family and friends think she's very lucky to have him, even though they know about his escapades. Magda won't say a critical word about him or her relationship. Instead she spends a fortune on clothes and cosmetics trying to keep him interested, and is forever at her GP's with a range of stress-related complaints. She doesn't know she's got the right to complain, to reflect. She's too dependent on him and what her friends think.

can be a problem, especially if your partner uses social pressure to add a gloss to his or her own anxiety about having their security threatened. Eileen, after her children had left home, had decided that she wanted to go back to work because she had time on her hands. There was some resistance from her husband but she persisted:

'The trouble was that I loved being back in the swing of things; I found that I'd missed a lot. I'd missed the company of other people, being part of a team. It was nice to have more to do with men for example and working with them; I'd forgotten how much fun it can be talking, flirting a little, dreaming a little. My husband hit the roof and became paranoid and jealous, accusing me of having affairs, the lot. He accused me of neglecting him and our home life, and he made me feel very guilty. He just would not give up and eventually I decided that it wasn't worth it and so I gave up the job.'

Eileen was simply trying to pick up the threads of experiences from which she had been cut off during the years that she was a housewife. Actually, what she was doing was healthy; most of us have unfinished business to do outside our routine roles and we grow as individuals if we can complete the learning we need. All too often our intimate relationships can cut us off from these levels of experience, with the result that in certain key respects we stay stuck where we were when we stopped dealing with other people.

Eileen needed space and time to pick up where she'd left off years earlier. She hadn't set out to have an affair; far from it. But she did need to re-establish a sense of herself as an attractive person which meant re-working her relationships with men. She needed to find out more about men and gain confidence in her ability to manage them. Her husband used social pressure to justify the fact that he felt threatened by her actions and Eileen unfortunately believed him. Inside she also felt very guilty seeing him so distressed and unsure of himself; she felt she was destroying his sense of security and couldn't see that perhaps he too needed to have his stability questioned.

Many people worry also about the effect any changes they make may have on their families, and sometimes partners can play on this. I'm reminded of one family in which the middle-aged mother wanted to change and do things for herself. Initially her husband was very negative and used every emo-

A best-case scenario

Janice was fortunate when she began to explore herself because of her strong relationship with Frank: 'Frank trusted me and this helped me a lot when I became middle-aged. I had led a very protected life and had always held men in awe. I was a bit of a fool and easily charmed. When I went back to work it was a close call in the beginning because I was nearly swept off my feet by one of the office charmers. I talked it over with Frank and that helped me to keep my feet on the ground. Now, five years on, I know a lot more about men and I can handle them without complications.'

tional manipulation in the book to stop the process; he accused her of being selfish, mentally disturbed, immature, the lot. He especially questioned her love for their children and accused her of wanting to break up the family. It got quite nasty and she was on the verge of leaving him when her teenage son asked what was wrong. (She wasn't the open kind and all the friction until then had been confined to whispered conversations behind the bedroom door.) To her surprise, when she told him what was going on, he turned round and told her that he thought she was absolutely right, that he'd always felt she'd lived too much in her husband's shadow. Encouraged, she became more open about what she felt. When her husband saw that there was some support for her side of things he got a shock and began to start thinking about things for himself. In time he actually came round to her way of thinking and between them they were able to work out a new set of compromises.

Relationships can change for the better if you focus on the relevant issues. Problems and disagreements aren't necessarily bad things, they can be clues to deeper personal issues, and tackling them can help you to develop and grow. It can help you to learn how to express yourself and your dream-map better, and in this we all need practice.

Just as our partners can block our development, so we can block our own exploration of ourselves and our relationships by obscuring the nature of the challenges involved. We can be

---

What not to do

Being jealous, resentful, possessive, making your partner feel guilty, showing unreasonable anger – these are some of the ways people try to contain changes in their partners. But we all use them at least some of the time and they are a natural part of relating. Where they cause trouble is when they block or stop the process of intimacy. On their own, they can be useful clues to internal emotional states; jealous people, for example, are often frustrated with their own patterns of coping and take out their resentments on their partners who are trying to make changes. In trying to stop their partners' activity, all they are doing is trying to maintain their own stability and put off their own development. If you feel these things often, or if your partner thinks they're getting out of hand, it's time to play Sherlock Holmes on yourself. If this doesn't work, get help. In the long run they will harm you as much as your partner.

---

blind like Magda and positively refuse even to consider the need to re-examine ourselves and our relationships, or we can hunt around for someone or something to blame as Wendy did at the onset of her troubles. Some people are aware of the need to explore their compromises yet fool themselves that they have exhausted all the options after several attempts at rebellion.

Take Bruce for example. He is in his late forties. He has been successful in his career and is both intelligent and sensitive. He's into what he thinks of as his second marriage. His first failed and, wary of commitment and the risk of making another mistake, he's been living with his partner for five years. She's also a professional woman and they get on well – much better, he feels, than he did with his first wife. He has a loose agreement with his partner about seeing other people and both have been discreetly involved in other affairs. But he's not happy and he suspects she isn't either. He's drinking too much, he says, but lacks the will or the energy to do anything about it. He wonders what he'll find if he cuts down. Sometimes Bruce feels he's as trapped by this modern second marriage as he was by the first, perhaps more so, but he can't blame the marriage or his loss of freedom any more. He's had his freedom and still, theoretically, has it – so what's wrong?

When he looks at his life he sees that he is still getting through by observing a series of rituals. Whereas before his life was structured by his married life – getting home, fetching the kids, visits to the parents – now with his new, freer, lifestyle he is observing different rituals, but rituals all the same. Bruce is convinced that his problem is that he hasn't found the right woman although even that idea is beginning to lose its attraction; he's had several other relationships and nothing seems to work or hang together for long enough to be meaningful.

Bruce is blocking his own development by consoling himself with the fact that he is a rebel and by blotting out his anxieties through drinking. I think he has a problem with asserting himself in relationships but he won't accept this. I've seen him cope with stress at work and he does it well. What he can't cope with is the stress of relating. As he puts it himself, he suffers more anxiety when Gina his partner calls him on the phone than anything that the chairman of the board can throw at him. If Gina calls, he literally breaks into a sweat at the thought of dealing with her. And why? Not because she's an especially difficult person but because in her own way she has a far greater effect on Bruce than anyone else does. She has a power over him that can literally make or break his day. And worse, Bruce knows it's not just her – anyone he gets into an intimate relationship with has the same effect. Yet he absolutely refuses to explore the issue.

It's much easier these days to fool ourselves that we are exploring our personalities by simply going through the rituals of rebelling as Bruce has. There's much more freedom in relationships now, much more acceptance of the need to find yourself, but it seems to me that we still have a long way to go towards understanding the full complexity of the problems, let alone trying to solve them. Many people today fool themselves into believing they've found the solutions when they're only beginning to explore the problems.

Relationships have always been a matter of seeking compromises and midlife has always been a time when compromises could be reviewed. The form that these compromises take varies from generation to generation, and in the past there was far less tolerance of people wanting to rebel overtly against the *status quo*. People were much more inclined to settle for a degree of companionship in their relationships as opposed to wanting to explore their relationships. Middle-aged people today are much more likely to want to delve deeper into the possibilities of both self-discovery and fulfilment and of making the most of their intimate relationships.

THE FIVE STEPS TO HEALTHY RELATING

There are five key ingredients that help to make a relationship healthy. By focusing on these you can help your relationship and at the same time get to know yourself better.

1 *Establish your individuality*
   One of the most important factors in the development of a healthy personality involves being able to develop a strong sense of personal, individual identity and autonomy. We saw in the last chapter how important it is for a growing child to learn how to think and to rebel for itself, to be able adequately to tackle the complexities of life. A large part of the development of this skill comes from dealing with reality in all its complexity, and learning to take responsibility for your own actions and thoughts, and this can be a very difficult thing to do if society, your partner and yourself conspire to help you avoid facing the challenge.

   One of the effects of the division of labour based on gender-role that characterizes relationships in our society is that women are traditionally dependent on men, and this can make it hard for both people to establish their own autonomy. If you're dependent on your partner for your economic needs, if you're spending most of your time looking after your children and the home, there's little room to test out your own need to get involved in life and living as a person outside these constraints. Your horizons are narrowed at all levels; often your friends are people in similar circumstances to yourself – parents of your children's friends, for example.

   One of the most important prerequisites for a good relationship is that it should allow for the development of a proper sense of personal worth and autonomy in the

Annette and Ron

Annette: 'I only really began to get to know myself at 48, after I got divorced. I suddenly became the bread-winner, and although it was incredibly tough, it turned me into my own person. Previously it was always Ron who dealt with any problems, and I now see that I used to make it worse because instead of going out and doing it myself, I used to nag him and criticize the way he handled things. Doing it myself made me realize how protected I'd been as a woman. Yes, there are times I wish for the old days when I had a man around to hide behind, but if I could go back I'd never want to take that role again.'

Ron: 'Since we split up we've actually become friends, perhaps for the first time. I can talk to her about things previously I used to hide from her. Say if I was worried about a problem, I'd never tell her about it because all she'd do was put more pressure on me and I'd always feel that I'd get it wrong anyway, not deal with it to her satisfaction. Some of the time it was my fault; I always used to feel that dealing with problems was a man's job.'

partners. We have to respect our partner's differences and try not to tie him or her to our own or society's ideas of what he or she should be. We need to recognize that one of the main challenges of relating is to be able to get past these expectations and fixations. Far too many people are in relationships – or want to be – to escape from being alone and autonomous. We use our relationships to escape from facing up to who or what we are; we have no faith in our ability to cope without our social and relational supports, and this can have skewed our original compromises. People sometimes think that autonomy means being alone, and while this can sometimes be the case, much more is involved; it means that you can think for yourself and make your own decisions, if necessary alone. It also means that you respect the other person's right to do the same thing.

2 *Develop friendship*

Closely related to this issue of autonomy is the question of friendship. Friendship is the basis of most of our relationships and healthy intimate relationships need to be based on friendship more than most. When you look again at your intimate relationships, or if you're looking for a relationship in the first place, it's worth spending some time on this question of friendship. Actually, ordinary friendships often contain a good deal more respect for individuality than do intimate ones, and the reason is usually because they are based on a desire to know the other person and to be known without all the social trappings that are involved in intimacy. Intimate relationships are all too often based on anything but friendship: sexual attraction, the need to be in a relationship, social pressure, for example. Ideally intimacy should grow out of friendship – it's rare for friendship to grow out of intimacy. People are sometimes so needy of being in a relationship that they get involved in intimacy without getting to know the person first. So even if you've been married or have lived together for a long time, you may still not know one another as friends, as people. Take a look at your partner; if you were not involved with him or her, would you want them as a friend? If the answer is No then it's time to find out why.

3 *Examine your ideas about love*

We all need to be loved. But what is love? We have a social definition defined by the appearance of being loved. We

---

Friends for life

A network of friends is the best guarantee of getting through life successfully. They can help you spread your needs around instead of focusing them all on one person, and they can serve as a sounding-board for new ideas, thoughts and feelings you may want to explore.

  They also give you support and confidence, help you get a better perspective on your problems and yourself, and will even help you to live longer.

have signs and symbols that we use to express this. But there is more to love than these symbols. Love is also about being known in the fullest sense of the word: sexually, emotionally and as a person. We only learn about ourselves and others by exploring the various aspects of our personalities in a relationship. Huge chunks of our personalities lie hidden away, unexplored and unexamined, in our dream-maps and how we relate helps to referent, to give shape and meaning to this map. Being known and loved helps to make the map a reality.

How do you love? How do you show your affection? how would you like to be loved? These questions are important guides to what may be missing in a relationship. There are few avenues in life outside our intimate relationships where we can be known and loved. I'm not talking here simply about sexuality – although that is involved – but rather about the range of means we have of showing and receiving love. Love isn't just about being good in bed, it also means being able to be affectionate, to cuddle, comfort, touch and caress – to show that you care. If you can't do these things – can't change – then maybe you need to find out why before you go off and find someone else.

4 *Explore your emotions*

Intimate relationships should ideally be gender-free oases where there is space, time and openness to delve deeply into yourself and your partner. When we talk about having our dream-maps fulfilled, this is what we mean. Intimate relating is about exploring ideas, thoughts, feelings and, most of all, emotions. We express an enormous amount of who we are as unique emotional individuals in these areas. So, if they don't form a part of relating, it means that an important and vital part of ourselves remains unworked and un-referenced.

Emotions are the source of a great deal of creativity both in the sense of, say, being imaginative or having good ideas, and in the sense of providing vital clues to the deeper reaches of ourselves. Expressing intimate emotions, managing and dealing with emotions, lies at the core of healthy relating. More trouble is caused by unexplored and unexpressed emotions than by almost anything else. Getting upset, getting angry, crying, talking about our hurts, anxieties and fears is a vital part of healthy functioning, both psychologically and physically. The body needs to release tension to complete its rest–activity coping cycles. When you've been angry, tense or upset, you need to download to compensate, otherwise it stays locked inside you. The more positive emotions need to receive the same treatment; your body and mind also need an outlet for happiness, joy, excitement and pleasure. You need to give and receive care and affection, to sing and dance, to do mad things from time to time.

Sharing emotions is a delicate business. You have to be patient and thoughtful with emotions – again for your own sake as much as your partner's. Emotions need time and space. You need to be able to talk out what is inside. Misunderstandings need time to be sorted out; men and women talk different languages sometimes, and different people mean different things by the same words – we all have private languages and they need to be shared in order to make a relationship work. Often when we first start talking, for example, we don't easily express what we want to; the process takes time and effort. Just as the Eskimos have many words for 'snow' where we have one, so we need to develop our emotional vocabularies. This isn't just about your immediate and physical sexual needs, it's also about your past feelings, about confidences, hurts, upsets, disappointments and about good things too, things you liked, moments you treasured, sadnesses, memories, relationships you never completed, dreams that were worked on perhaps but not finished. There is a wealth of this kind of material inside each of us and most of us want to share it.

Many of our deeper emotions are expressed through our sexuality, which is why it's so important to us. If you feel that your partner is responsive to your sexual needs, it can be one of the most rewarding experiences. Quite apart from the physical sensations involved, it helps you gain trust and confidence and can unlock some of the wealth of feeling inside your dream-map. Sexual incompatibility is often given as a reason for relationships breaking up and for why people have affairs during midlife.

Many issues are involved in sharing emotions over and above the ability simply to talk about things. After all, many couples can talk, but some don't listen and some don't talk about the things that really matter. Most of us have very little

Good one, Linda

'After my menopause I re-discovered my sexuality and this caused me a lot of difficulty because it was as if I was a different person. I felt excited to be alive. The problems came because I didn't know what to do with it. My needs had changed. I wanted passion in my life. Talking to my husband about it was a total waste of time. He was of the quick-roll-in-the-hay-and-fall-asleep kind. So I had an affair. Actually two affairs. They saved my emotional life because through them I was really able to open up and find myself.

'Then I stopped having affairs; I didn't need them – I'd found what I wanted and I couldn't take the guilt. These sexual experiences unlocked parts of me I'd buried away. I weighed up my life and decided that I liked my home and family, even loved my husband enough to stay with him. I didn't want to break up my relationship – just make it work better for me. So I did. I went back to university as a mature student, did many of the things I'd always wanted to do

'Then it occurred to me that if I'd used my passion, my sexuality, to explore things, maybe I could get my husband to go through the same process. Not that I wanted him to have an affair (although it would probably have helped him) but maybe I could get him to talk about his sexual needs more, you know, his fantasies and the like. Well, it worked. It was in fact unbelievable. He was so pleased that I wanted to know about him that it finally occurred to him to wonder about me. Who would have believed that we'd end up in our fifties behaving like a couple of teenagers in our bedroom. Best of all though was that through all this, I think we found each other. Life is so different now, we talk and share and we have, I think, found what love is really about.'

experience of proper talking and proper listening. To do this you need to trust – trust that you will be understood and trust that there will be time to explore what you talk about.

5 *Clarify what you want from your relationships*
The last step is perhaps the hardest to take because it involves taking a long, honest look at you and your relationship. Is your relationship a kind of security blanket; do you
huddle together against the outside world? Are you terrified
of being alone? There is nothing wrong with these things so
long as you know what you want and are satisfied and of
course the same goes for your partner. If you want more,
though, you have to go and get it. After all, you're middle-
aged, it's your right.

+-----------+
| THE |
| KEY | *Exploring and self-discovery*
| ISSUE |
+-----------+

The common factor that runs through these steps is the ability
to explore. In fact, it seems to me that each of us has so much
exploring to do in a lifetime, it sometimes surprises me how
much time people waste on avoiding tackling the issues of
getting to know their partners and getting to know themselves.
And this is where I think we need to focus some of our
rebellious energy. It takes a lot to rebel against convention,
against your partner's or your own reluctance to look deeper
into things. Healthy relating involves making a commitment to
wanting to explore yourself and your partner.

Far too many people are afraid of doing this. They are afraid
of questioning, of talking about deep personal matters and
they're afraid of emotion. Many people regard emotions with
suspicion, they regard expressing emotion as evidence of
weakness, of mental illness or instability. Think about the
states in which so many people reach midlife – overwrought,
unhealthy, depressed, bored, frustrated, unfulfilled. All the
symptoms that are regularly trotted out to characterize midlife
are symptoms not of midlife, but of unfulfilled and unquestioned
emotional needs. Little wonder that some women react badly
to menopause and that middle-aged men complain of sexual
boredom and impotence; these are not just the consequences
of midlife processes but all too often of failed communication.

A person wanting to try to forge new compromises with his
or her partner has to go out on a limb, especially if the partner
is unwilling to engage in the same process. Obviously if your

partner can't cope with what you're trying to do, or if he or she won't get involved, you have to consider leaving or forming other relationships. There is no perfect relationship and sometimes you may have to consider having several relationships that help you tap into your needs. I don't imply here having a set of sexual partners, but rather, if necessary, having a set of relationships that allows you the scope to get at the person you are. Living alone or living some of the time alone is also a useful option for some people, especially if they do not easily communicate with their partners.

No matter what option you choose, the ultimate aim is to get on with what you have to do for yourself – that is, self-discovery, hopefully within a relationship but if necessary, alone. Bear in mind that relationships are complex entities and I don't think anyone has a copyright on what makes a successful relationship.

Some tips

- Do take risks, try new things, examine, open up, lose your inhibitions.
- Do look at how you express yourself, how you get angry and show affection.
- Do ask questions about yourself and your relationships.
- Do learn to believe in yourself. Take part in life.
- Don't be too afraid of what people will think.
- Don't hide behind your relationships.
- Don't blame others for your own problems.
- Don't be afraid to confront and make changes.
- Don't leave it too late.

CHAPTER SIX

Changes in the Family

As adults, especially as we get older, we tend to look back on our family life at home in much the same way as we may look back on our school days and remember them as being so much simpler and straightforward than the pressured and anxious lives we lead as grown-ups. If we scratch the surface though and think a bit deeper about what life was like in our family as we grew up, most of us come up with a more complex picture. For many of us, family life was a mixed bag of good and bad which has left both pleasant and not-so-pleasant memories. Mostly we tend to remember only the good times and forget those that were difficult, the more so if we had good relationships with our parents. We almost certainly idealize our own family life if it was generally good and demonize it if it was generally bad. Very few of us have an accurate perspective of our own family life. We remember it from the perspective of a child and this stays with us for most of our lives.

It is difficult for anybody to get an accurate picture of family life because we always play a set role in our families and it's hard to generalize from outside this role. In fact as we live out our lives we have access to three separate perspectives on family life: when we are growing up in our families, when we are parents with our own families, and when we are grand-parents. We rarely, however, have to put these perspectives into some kind of order.

Each of the perspectives we gain provides us with such powerful impressions that we may be overwhelmed by them and find it hard to consider other perspectives. This is natural because we hold the roles that we play for so long that they become ingrained into our thinking at the time and stay as such in our memories later when we reflect or think back. It's hard when we're children to think about family life from our parents' perspective and it's not so easy to do the reverse when we are parents ourselves.

Why am I telling you all this? Mainly because one of the biggest challenges that we face during midlife is to re-examine these roles of child and parent and try to put the perspectives together. At midlife we are the link between the generations above and below us, and how we proceed has important effects for them and us. Part of the process of fulfilling our dreams is to be able to know people properly while there is still time. At midlife we have a rare opportunity to get to know them better and perhaps build closer and lasting relationships; as we find our real selves as individuals we may also find out who they are.

Naturally, few of us re-examine our perspectives out of choice. Mostly it happens as a side effect of some other pressure or change. There are a number of ways in which we can become aware of the need to re-think our roles within the family and our ideas about family life. One way is through guilt or anxiety about any changes we may want to make as a result of becoming middle-aged. Let's say for example that you've done a certain amount of thinking about yourself and decided that you're not happy with the way you are. One of the first things you'll worry about, especially if you've still got children living at home, is the effect your new thinking will have on your children. Will they accept the new you? Will the changes you want to make disrupt your family life? If you have no children or if they've grown up and left home, you may instead worry about the effects any change will have on your parents. Will they approve of what you want to do? Will they support or condemn you?

Often though there are more practical reasons for having to modify our understanding of family life. One of the important factors that help to give shape to the midlife challenges we face is that for most of us midlife arrives at about the same time that our children are going through adolescence or early adulthood. Dealing with young people in general can have the same effect. Another factor with practical consequences is that at the same time our own parents may find themselves in changed circumstances – they may have retired, fallen ill, lost their partners or be suffering disabilities from old age and need help.

The result is that at midlife we are often faced with two major challenges to our perspectives: adjusting to the changes that are taking place in our own children or other young people in our lives, and adjusting to changes taking place in our parents. These challenges are of course in addition to everything else that takes place during midlife and which sometimes obscures the crucial family changes that are occurring over the same period.

COPING WITH YOUNG PEOPLE

One of the most difficult tasks a parent has is to cope with the changes that the children undergo as they progress through their adolescence and engage in various forms of rebellion. Part of the difficulty lies in the fact that much of what happens takes place in your own back yard, within the confines of your family life. It is a little like letting a stranger into your inner sanctum or like realizing that someone you previously took for granted has changed and you have to get to know them all over again. Suddenly the calm and tranquillity of home life can be turned upside down by one of its members. It can be stimulating but it can also cause enormous tension.

There are a number of ways in which adolescent changes and rebellion can have an effect on a middle-aged parent: they can challenge the pre-existing relationship that the child has with the parent; they can raise disturbing personal issues for the parent; and they can interfere with the relationship between the parents. These effects are of course interconnected. Usually both parents play a role in child rearing and the child slowly but surely becomes a player in the adults' relationship.

Children know a great deal about their parents and the nature of their parents' relationship – more than they can talk about or express. They are nearly always involved in a range of power and personality battles within family life. Their involvement may be slight during childhood but it tends to increase during adolescence.

Adolescents frequently do more than simply challenge parental authority. Much more is involved because in so doing, they inevitably challenge the personalities and methods of coping of their parents. Because adolescents know more about their parents than anyone else, they are armed with very delicate information. A younger child may be aware of the same information but teenagers are more likely – if provoked or if they feel desperate enough – to say things that no one else would.

Adolescent attempts to rebel and assert their independence can cause problems in the relationship between parents because sometimes the child focuses on conflicts that already exist between partners as a means of getting their own point across. A child may use the support of one parent against the other; one parent may take advantage of the conflict to vent on the other feelings previously hidden. This can be very upsetting, and how disruptive of the parental relationship it is depends on how effectively the parents manage the challenge.

We have to remember that this challenge often comes in the wake of another effect brought on by the onset of adolescence. As we saw earlier, observing your children go through adolescent struggles often re-awakens memories of your own adolescent experiences. Watching your teenager trying to find his or her way in new relationships, trying to come to terms with new emotions, growth and the general turmoil of adolescence can remind you of dormant, unresolved issues that you have still to sort out for yourself. If at the same time your teenager is challenging you and your relationship (which you may also be questioning yourself) and saying painful but insightful things, it can feel like you've walked into a nightmare. So in a sense you may be more vulnerable to the challenges that they force on you when all they are doing (in their own minds) is questioning your values and your authority. Moreover, it's not just a question of having to deal with your own adolescent children – much the same kind of issues can crop up when dealing with younger people in any circumstance. If for example you have to deal with nephews or nieces, friends' children, people you work with or teach, the challenges are essentially the same.

There is another way that family circumstances can change during midlife when your grown-up children finally leave home. Obviously if you still have growing children at home, the impact of the 'empty nest' effect can be lessened, but for many people a child's leaving home introduces a lot of new challenges that have to be faced. The structure of family life may alter significantly. Where there may have been three or four people in the family for you to focus on, suddenly there is just you and your partner, or just you on your own. The presence of children, especially adolescent children, can take up a lot of family time and focus attention away from the more personal aspects of the interaction between the partners or distract you from focusing on your own problems.

If you've invested a lot of your time and energy in your role as a parent and minimized your role as a person or as a partner in a relationship, the sudden absence of a child can create a major psychological gap in your life. Someone once put it to me referring to her husband, 'After the kids had gone it felt like waking up in the morning to find you've been living with a stranger.'

When a grown-up child leaves home you can also find the role you have with your child changing. You will no longer be the focus of your children's lives, no longer the local authority figure or the person they turn to when they're in trouble. You may not even see them very often. When, later, a spouse and grandchildren enter the picture, your role may have to change yet again.

Each one of these changes can have an effect on your equilibrium. This can either distress you and intensify your feelings about getting old and losing touch, or it can jolt you into doing something about it.

What to do: five steps to staying in touch with young people

Few people respond well to challenges to their authority, beliefs and personality, or to feelings of loneliness and isolation. When looking for a way of communicating with the young people involved, there are a number of points to bear in mind:

1 *Take a look at the perspective you have of young people*
Most adults quite naturally adopt a perspective of the young people in their lives based on the preceding years during which they were growing up. Older adults in general tend to think they are wiser and maturer than younger people anyway. The difficulty is that the roles that adults play, especially parents, are often hard to change. Parents often

adhere rigidly to their role as parents without realizing that they have to change and develop new roles as their children grow up. When you've got a toddler or a young child you need to be authoritative and strict, and they will naturally see you as being all-powerful. But from their adolescence on you've gradually got to change this role. As your teenager develops, he or she needs to get to know you as a person, not just as a mother or a father. By the time he or she is a young adult this need is very strong. It can help your child have a better, broader perspective about you as a person, about life and about relationships.

We have to try to see that there is more to being a parent than just being a father or a mother. Far too few parents bother getting to know their children as growing, developing people unless they have an area of interest to share or unless the child fits into a need the parent might have. How often have you heard parents say that they felt close to their sons or daughters when they were a certain age but not at other times? How many times do you hear about a father only taking an interest in his son or daughter when he or she is old enough to provide companionship? Or a mother complaining about their child who no longer wants to play mother's little helper? Younger children can be adorable, but the real challenge is to handle the gawky, difficult and rebellious teenager who is in a process of change at about the same time as you are.

Older adults sometimes struggle to accept the rights and perspectives of younger people. Young people may be inexperienced but this doesn't alter the fact that they will change as they age, and as they do so they will evolve their own ways of doing things. Just as you may have things to teach them, so they may teach you. The more insecure we are as individuals, the more we cling to our middle-aged roles and status and the more rigid our perspectives become.

2 *Don't inflict your problems on your children*
Dealing with a young person may make you feel impotent or angry, and you may take it very personally and turn all your hostility and anger on your children or onto your partner. I have seen few people as bitterly angry as a parent towards a rebellious teenager, as if years of stored-up bitterness and resentment has been unleashed on the

Jeff

'I was what you'd call a routine parent to my teenage son from my first marriage. I did my job; I cared. I was a good parent, but I didn't know him very well. There was a distance between us: we only played out our roles. So I tried talking to him, you know, man-to-man stuff. Forget it. How do you communicate with someone whose entire range of conversation consists of 'yeah', 'dunno', and who is obsessed with the lyrics to every song Alice in Chains ever recorded? Then one day we were staying over at a friend's house who is also a father and about my own age. We were lounging around after lunch and his friend had a synthesizer and liked rock music and began to play. Eventually my son got interested and joined in, and watching the two of them mess around on the synthesizer overwhelmed me with jealousy for a moment. I saw that this bloke treated my son differently from the way I did. Obviously it wasn't his son, so he treated him like anyone else. He didn't have to be a father, to play the role. He was relaxed and at ease and open about what he knew and didn't know. This could've happened with anybody but it just hit me and I decided to do something about it; to stop trying to be just a good father, but to be more myself.'

What was important about Jeff's insight was that it came at a crucial time in his own development and acted as a kind of catalyst for helping him to change the perspective he had of his son. He was able to see too that he had been far too preoccupied with his own midlife *angst*. He realized that he needed to work at the relationship he had with his son and find a way to communicate with him, even if it meant taking an interest in his kind of music. The music wasn't the issue; showing interest and respect for difference was. Jeff took piano lessons and started playing music with his son; it was only then that he began to get a perspective of what the music meant to his son. Previously he had only been concerned with his perspective. He didn't change his feelings about the music but it didn't matter.

child-who-is-no-longer-a-child. Many young people who leave home too early often do so to escape from this kind of resentment and anger.

Be careful to separate out your problems from theirs. It's often difficult to keep a healthy perspective in the face of these challenges but it is very important to understand what is happening; let them get on with their lives and their problems while you get on with yours.

3 *Share perspectives*

No one is perfect. No one has a perfect relationship. We all make compromises and adjustments to the challenges of life. By midlife we've usually created a kind of compromised, marginal existence for ourselves. Everybody does this. But young people are more idealistic, more inclined to believe that perfection exists and can be achieved, just as we were when we were their age. This is the basis of their rebellion against us as older adults and parents. And in different ways both are right: we are right to have made compromises; young people are right to believe that there is more to life than these compromises and that things can change. After all, that is precisely the issue we should be facing in midlife anyway!

It is vital that we don't lose track of the fact that the core of their criticisms or challenges is frequently worth thinking about. All too often we get so upset or angry with them that we swamp them with a deluge of defensive self-justifications of the after-all-we've-done-for-you kind which miss the point. The key task is to be able to cope with the young person's perspective in a way that helps him or her to maintain a viable relationship with you. All too often the way parents react to their teenagers creates a distance between them, and the children enter adulthood without the level of emotional support they need from their parents. Adolescence can be just as traumatic for the child as for the adults involved. What we need to do is find a balance, pick out what is useful and good in the relationship, and give our children the space and time to find out that they too will have to make compromises. Sharing our own ideas can help too by showing them that we don't have all the answers and that it's never a matter of anyone winning, but rather of accepting differences.

Make my day, Kate

Kate's mother and father were constantly involving their children in their personal conflicts. Kate was the youngest of a family of three children and each child in turn had played a crucial role in the parents' power structure. Each parent had formed a close relationship with one special child. When each left home there had been problems as the respective parent latched onto a new supporter in the family. Both parents were enormously competitive and self-involved. They didn't get on well together and basically only stayed married for the children's sake.

When Kate's sister had left home, her father had switched his attentions to Kate and they became very close. Her mother had been experiencing a difficult menopause at the time, had had a bit of a crisis and 'solved' the problem by losing interest in the home. She was out most of the time and the task of looking after her husband and providing companionship for him fell onto Kate who was then 15.

Kate was flattered and responded gratefully; she'd always felt left out before and secretly resentful of her older siblings. This arrangement worked for a long time. Even after Kate left home and went to university, she would still pop in at home three or four times a week to see if her father was all right. When Kate was 23 however she fell in love with a fellow student and the problem started. She felt enormously guilty about leaving her father to fend for himself and this wasn't helped by his reaction of hurt and bitterness. Eventually things got so bad she stopped going home because she couldn't cope with his recriminations. Ultimately Kate's father had to sort himself out and tackle the relationship – or lack of one – he had with his wife. Only then was he in a position to try and rescue his relationship with his children.

Single parents

Sharing perspectives is also important for single parents, but there are one or two other points that need to be considered. Because you are the sole parent you can sometimes feel that you are more responsible for your children than are ordinary parents, and it can be harder to keep a healthy perspective about things; how much dare you do for yourself? Many single parents feel guilty about their own broken relationships which, if occurring during midlife, can increase a sense of personal failure. And there can be the added burden of helping the children cope with the change at the same time as trying to do so themselves.

Tanya, for example, was dominated by her teenage daughter and felt guilty for not providing her with a proper home. She had real problems in sorting out her own midlife problems simply because her daughter wouldn't let her be: in order to be free and develop, Tanya had to re-define her relationship with her daughter, and this involved getting a better perspective of what the issues were and what her own rights as a person were. When she did, with professional help, the relationship between the two of them improved enormously, largely because Tanya no longer allowed her daughter to blame her for everything that was wrong in her life; they could get past the guilt block and get on with their relationship.

4 *Keep in touch*
As we saw in the last chapter, friendship is the basis of most intimate relationships. It's vital to retain something of your love and contact with young people in your life. Sometimes you just have to let them be to find themselves and their place in life. Disagree by all means, agree to differ, but don't stop loving and showing your interest in them. You could also look again at how you may have helped or hindered them in the process of growing up to be an individual; it's never too late to mend fences.

5 *Believe in yourself*

It's just as important not to lose sight of the fact that you're also an individual with rights. Sometimes coping with young people at the same time as midlife may be sapping your belief in yourself. It can be easy to give in to the relentless logic and conviction that is showered upon you. Don't – this is where sharing your fears with close friends can really help to stabilize your equilibrium.

AGEING PARENTS

As if coping with young people isn't tough enough, there's often another event that can turn your world upside down during midlife: the return of your own parents into your life. What usually happens is that for a variety of reasons your parents may suddenly need you in ways that they haven't before. This time though the roles may be reversed; instead of being in the needy, dependent role you played as a child, it often happens that you have now to play the powerful, providing one. Suddenly you have to rethink and rework your relationship with your parents, and this can be a difficult task depending on how close you've been to your parents and how good a relationship you've had with them in the past.

During young adulthood we get involved in relationships of our own, with our partners and with our children, usually at the expense of the relationship we had earlier with our parents. Out of sight can sometimes mean out of mind, and the relationships we have within our own nuclear family often become more immediate and more intimate than those we have with our own parents. They are around, certainly, but with nothing like the kind of power and influence they held previously.

One consequence of this is that we tend to encapsulate our own childhood experiences and our feelings about our parents. We are so focused on the immediate demands of our lives that we seldom have much time to continue developing our relationships with our parents. In fact, to some extent, we withdraw from them; we relate, but we do so at a distance. We lose track, as it were, of them as people, largely because for us they were never 'ordinary people'; they were always Mum and Dad, special, powerful people. We related to them (even in adversity, even in our rebellions) in ways we seldom relate to other people.

Of course, some people do continue to track their relationships with their parents but I think by and large this is relatively rare: most of us are too preoccupied with our ongoing lives. I think it is one of the tragedies of modern life that there is little appreciation of the need to maintain relational contact between generations.

Although we may encapsulate our memories of home life, the effects of our upbringing remain with us. In fact, you could say that we spend a good deal of our adult lives getting over the effects of our childhood relationships with our parents. Our parents' values, ideas and ideals remain ever present and help to shape our own thoughts and behaviours. The problem is that what we learn in relationships with our parents is one-sided and to some extent out of context. And because the learning and the memories are encapsulated, it is very difficult for us to think constructively about them. One result is that we often hold on to attitudes and beliefs and patterns of rebellion for years without really being aware of the context in which they arose.

Then, out of the blue (or so it seems), old age catches up with our parents. They may fall ill and they may need to be looked after. Sometimes they may find themselves alone and need company. Whatever the reason, you have to get involved with them again. They may have to come and live with you or you may have to spend more time with them.

Trevor

When I was 32 my father and I were sitting in a car park waiting for my mother. For a variety of reasons my father – then middle-aged – started chatting to me about his personal life and struggles. Luckily my mother was late and for three hours (she was very late) my dad opened up like he had never done before – and never did again. What he told me during this time was precious to me because it put so many of the things I didn't understand about him into perspective, and I was able to see him in a new light as a person with problems just like mine. My only regret was that I wished that he had done this when I was 19 or 20 and we were struggling with our relationship.

What to do: four steps to staying in touch with older people

Coping with the needs and demands of elderly parents can be a very difficult experience. We feel guilty if we do too little, worry in case we're being unfair, get angry if they demand too much and so on. Friction can develop over these issues and not just between you and your parents but between you and the rest of your family. There are several points that need to be attended to and which can help to ease any difficulties that emerge.

1 *Get to know your parents as people (if they'll let you)*
How well do you know your parents as people? Most people still see their parents in the same way they did when they lived with them at home. It's only when your parents get older, retire, get divorced, widowed or fall ill that you may discover the limitations of the perspective you have of them. You may notice things about them for the first time which have probably been there all along. Sometimes you get the chance to see behind some of their attitudes, or behind ways they have of dealing with things that may have upset you or caused conflict in the past. You might see for example that strong attitudes masked a fear and insecurity, or a frailty that you could not have guessed at before.

These new insights can be deeply challenging and disturbing for us, the more so if we were used to seeing our parents as all-powerful figures of authority. Much also depends on how involved we have to get with them and whether this new involvement leads to deeper understanding or not.

Getting to know our parents is not an easy task. Sometimes there is a backlog of hurt and confusion on both sides. Sometimes the older generation can be hard to approach directly; they're not used to the kind of openness and dialogue that many present-day middle-aged people are used to. They don't see things in the same light. But there are ways through this impasse and in some respects it's up to us to find them if and when we can. The task is to try, again, to rebel against the backlog of roles and reactions we have established in the past.

2 *Protect your own individuality and autonomy*
If a parent needs constant help or needs to live with his or

her children, this can add an extra burden to the relationships in the family. Other family members may resent the
time and space that has to be given to elderly parents. It can
also be a source of friction between partners, especially, as
often happens, if the burden for coping falls on the woman.
Ageing parents can, in their own way, be as deeply challenging to a relationship as any of the other challenges you may
face at midlife.

Another problem is that ageing parents can become quite
self-centred (some may have always been) and demand a
great deal of your time and emotional energy. This may
worsen if they find themselves on their own. Sometimes
they can inadvertently – or even deliberately – break up a
relationship. Give them whatever help they may need, but
don't lose sight of the fact that you have a life to lead and
relationships of your own to run.

3 *Try to resolve your personal differences with your parents*
Most of us really do spend a good deal of our adult lives
recovering from our childhood relationships with our parents.
Usually we achieve this by getting away from our parents,
trying to escape their influence, if you like. As things stand,
this is sometimes all that you can do – escaping may give
you a chance to lead your own life, especially if you have
opinionated or dominating parents to contend with. This is
usually one of the reasons why their re-entry into their
middle-aged children's lives can cause such distress. It helps
enormously if you can tackle these issues beforehand. Sometimes just straight talking works; sometimes you need to take
a good look at what else may be going on in a relationship.
Where there's fear, there's conflict, and sometimes it may
need working on.

4 *Help your parents get on with their own lives*
Some older people need help in getting on with their own
lives. This is especially true when, say, one of them has
retired and is at a loss for something to do, or when one of
your parents has died and the other can't seem to get over
it. Getting them back on their feet is as important for you as
it is for them. Putting them in touch with other people of the
same age, getting them to stay active and involved with
people can work wonders for them and for you.

Ivor was distressed to find that his elderly father was planning to spend five or six months of the year with him and his family, and the same time with his sister's family. His father, a strong, dominating person had recently been widowed and had simply announced his intention without discussion as was his habit. Ivor had harboured enormous resentment against his father for as long as he could remember, and he'd struggled for years to live up to what he saw as his father's standards and expectations. Understandably he went through a kind of midlife crisis at the prospect and ended up taking anti-depressants to help him cope.

When we chatted about his father's impending visit (he'd spent the first five months with Ivor's sister) it was clear that there was unfinished emotional business for Ivor to attend to. He felt as if he'd been thrown back into his teens and was at a loss about what to do. There was however a way. What he had to do was to rebel against the old role he had played and the old emotions he felt, and try to find different ways of achieving what he wanted. Ivor realized that what he really wanted to do was to stand up for himself, tell his father what he felt, and get his father to find another solution. Plucking up courage, he went to see his father and told him exactly what he thought. There was a tremendous row and Ivor's father stormed out in a rage leaving Ivor feeling terribly guilty.

Despite this, the overall result was very satisfying. About a month after the argument his father phoned and asked to chat to him, and they went out to lunch together. His father was wary of Ivor and still fairly angry but he'd realized that the relationship needed to go on and that perhaps, after all, Ivor was right to feel the way he did. Slowly Ivor got to know his father a lot better and this helped fulfil at least one part of his dream-map: to have a decent relationship with his father in which they could explore their feelings for one another with respect instead of conflict and struggle.

| THE |
| KEY | *Children, parents and grandparents as people*
| ISSUE |

Clearly, from what we've been discussing so far, a lot can happen in the family at midlife. All these events present a similar challenge; they force us to re-think the roles we have been playing in our family. What this boils down to is that we have to start the process of trying to see the young people in our lives and our parents as people over and above the roles we have played with them. One of the problems in our society is that we not only move away from our parents or our children physically when we or they leave home, but we may also stop the process of getting to know them as people until need and necessity forces us to do so.

Under these circumstances family members remain purely role-figures for one another. They are wary of opening up and apprehensive about stepping outside their roles. Imagine how useful it could be for children if they had better communication with their parents, if they were aware of the difficulties and struggles their parents were going through at the same time as they themselves were struggling to find their place in the world.

There are no easy answers to the problems that come up but in my experience both as a parent and a therapist the key to managing the challenges successfully lies in the degree to

---

Some tips

- Share your thoughts, dreams, problems and ideas.
- Try doing new things together: don't just stick to the old family rituals. New activities give you new opportunities to get to know one another.
- Treat them as people not objects. Try to see them as potential new friends.
- Try talking about shared memories – you might be surprised to hear the other side of familiar, old stories.
- Be yourself and let them be themselves.

which the middle-aged person can be open about what is going on in his or her own life.

While it is important to get to know our parents and children as people, it is just as important that we give them the opportunity to get to know us as people too; just as they've played roles for us, so we have played roles for them. These changes in the family at midlife can effect the three generations of family members; all of whom may be trying to find their feet at the same critical time but for different reasons.

The changes in family structure that occur at midlife are easier to manage if you have already developed an ability to question the social roles you have learned to play. Holding on to older patterns of rebelling, holding on to old ways of gaining security and coping with conflict are signs that you're not facing up to what and who you are, and what you need to do for yourself and your family. Another factor we have to bear in mind is that by and large the challenges fall hardest on

---

Welcome to the rest of your life

Rita was under a great deal of pressure during her midlife. She found dealing with her parents a strain and she was constantly in conflict with her own grown-up children. The trouble was that she was almost completely artificial with them; she played roles and never let her defences down. She had created barriers between herself and the key people in her life precisely because no one knew what was going on inside her. They had no idea what she felt or thought, or what problems she was facing, simply because she believed in keeping everything under control. If her parents visited she ended up feeling stressed and tired. I suggested that her life would be a lot easier if these key people knew more about her, but for a long time she adamantly denied the need to take them into her confidence. When she did she got a big surprise. She finally discovered how much they really cared for who she was as a person; in fact they were much more open than she was and had all been waiting for her to get off the pedestal she'd put herself on.

women. Despite all you might read about men sharing in home life and family responsibilities, much of the burden of organizing family life still falls on women. Even if the woman in a relationship has a job, she's still charged with the responsibility of coping with the children and often with elderly parents too. For many women, their entire focus is on the family with the result that upheavals within it tend to fall on them, because they are there and because it is usually by social, if not mutual consent, their domain.

It's hard to find yourself if your role-burden is too great; you need help in coping to give yourself a chance to get your own work done. So when we think about what needs to be done in the family at midlife we have to do more than just change our perspective about our roles with our children or our parents; we have to look too at the perspective we hold of our partner and the stresses he or she may be undergoing.

CHAPTER SEVEN

Career Angst at Midlife

When you're a child, quite a lot of your thinking is directed towards what kind of career you will follow when you grow up. This focus is part of how you are taught to think about the Big World out there: little boys are taught to think in terms of male-orientated careers and little girls female-orientated careers. While much of your thinking revolves around the gender-based form your role in the world will take, the main ingredient of youthful thinking is the excitement of doing things 'out there'. Being a child can be frustrating; there are so many things you can't do, just because you're little, and not big, strong or clever enough to do the things that seem to make the world outside such an exciting place. You see your mum and dad going off to work and you envy them. Well, at least you envy them until you find out what schoolteachers, accountants, bus drivers or dentists actually do.

Most children dream about doing really exciting things when they grow up, like being a soldier, fireman or fighter pilot; fashion model, air hostess or film star. This dreaming is an important part of the dream-map we build up early on in life, and like everything else, as we grow older this dream has to be modified. There are all sorts of factors that limit and shape what careers we actually take up. Gender is one, education, personality, family and economic pressures, opportunity and plain luck are others.

Some people know from an early age what they want to do and go for it, but many people reach late adolescence with no clear idea in mind what they want to do in life, and often play around with several possibilities. Parental and social pressures

121

and economic opportunities combine to force us to make a choice. And most of the choices we make carry long-term commitments. It's hard once you've started accountancy or medicine or architecture or mechanical engineering to change your mind; once the choice is made, the career has a momentum of its own. This of course includes becoming a housewife which can require as much of a commitment as any other career.

Amidst all these pressures any uncertainty about what you really want to do gets lost or submerged by the ongoing demands of your chosen career. There is also tremendous social pressure not to change; people who change their careers too often or can't make up their minds what to do are typically regarded as unstable.

Building or creating a career can take up a major portion of your time, energy and interest. Of course, the process has its rewards, but these create their own momentum and pressure such that financial and personal security become vested in your career, which can make it hard to change or to leave. By the same token, threats to job security can be an important source of personal stress, and if you're constantly worried about your job you may never have the opportunity to think about doing something else.

CAREERS AT MIDLIFE

There are many reasons why there is often opportunity for reflection during the midlife period. Success, particularly financial success, or reaching a plateau in your career can create circumstances which allow you time to wonder if, after all, you're really satisfied with your career. Since, with most careers, your twenties are spent learning and qualifying and your thirties building up a base, there is a kind of natural rhythm to our economic cycles that dictates that it is usually in your forties that you get a chance to reflect properly. If your children leave home at the same time it may mean economic pressure and emotional pressure eases, which can give us space to re-evaluate career choice. Of course children leaving home can also create the opportunity for you to get started on a career that you've always wanted to follow.

There are two basic challenges that arise during this period.

The first concerns issues that arise within the job itself, and the second concerns broader issues relating to whether or not you want to be in your current job. Both test your ability to cope with change.

Status changes

There are many things that can happen in a person's career during midlife to create new challenges. Often you begin to realize that you are, after all, ageing, and while some careers reward you in terms of improved status and remuneration as you age, increasingly today the opposite happens and you can begin to feel that your age is a handicap. Sometimes you find yourself having to re-think the role you have always played at work: a lot of people struggle with adjusting to being a middle-aged person when they have been used to thinking of themselves and playing a role as someone young and up-and-coming.

Young adults intent on building a career naturally tend to build a role around competing with older people, trying to prove their worth within their company or organization. Some might have gained status and prestige by their ability to provide new ideas and new energy, others by their ability to break with tradition in order to achieve results in new ways. When you're older this may have to change, and you may have to develop other aspects of your skills and learn to play different roles. You may find yourself having to adjust to the fact that other people now see you as older and more staid, or having to learn to deal with younger people doing to you exactly what you used to do to older people. You may have to shift over from seeing yourself as a young Turk and adapt perhaps to a more guiding, moderating role as an older person. Now you're the teacher, no longer the bright young thing asking awkward questions. Some people find this difficult to cope with; sometimes middle-aged people can be quite fixed in their ways and ideas, and resent having to change them.

Don't however think of these challenges as being purely due to ageing. There can be economic and practical reasons why they come up at midlife. If for example you've spent your early adult years building up a business or career, it often happens that you will have reached a stage at which it is economically necessary for you to change your role at about the time you become middle-aged. I know many people who are really brilliant at starting up a company from scratch, putting in countless extra hours to develop markets to get the show on the road, but are quite useless at the administrative and managerial roles they are obliged to play when the start-up period is over and they are employing other people to do the legwork.

Economic cycles and thus career demands, just like life, change over time. Little remains static and part of dealing with the world out there involves coming to terms with these changes. Markets change, statuses can change; skills or talents that have worked for us at one time may not work at others, and we have to adjust to this.

One of the most important factors affecting the way we cope with challenges is how much of ourselves we have invested emotionally in our careers. Many people literally pour themselves into their career roles, be it bank manager or housewife, and seldom get the chance to reflect on whether this is healthy for them or their relationships. The careers we choose give us more than an income or status; they help us to feel part of life. We gain a degree of confidence and security from them. We also quite naturally put a great deal of our emotional needs into our careers which, if not fulfilled, can have a very devastating effect on our self-confidence. A lot of people invest too much in the role they play in their jobs and suffer when this is threatened because they haven't given themselves a chance to develop more fully as a person outside their job. When challenges come up in the work situation, they can be taken out of proportion and construed as more threatening than they really are.

These examples give you some idea of the kind of changes that can occur in careers around the midlife period. While they can add to the pressures that you are already experiencing, they can also act as an incentive to ask questions about the career compromises you have had to make in the past.

Career choice

The second issue that seems to be occurring more and more for middle-aged people nowadays is the question of career choice. This can arise in a number of different ways but always

Retirement and men

In the past it was men who most often experienced problems when they got close to retirement age and this may well be why the male menopause is traditionally thought to occur later than women's. After a lifetime pouring all their energies into their careers, suddenly men are faced with having to live life without their career support systems around them. They have to learn who they are as people without the help of company cars, secretaries and the like. It was men who went out to work and held demanding positions of power, and their situation was directly analogous to the situation which many women have to face when their children leave home; just like men at retirement, they have to learn to find themselves as people without the input they were previously used to. With changing times and as more women work and assume positions of power, women may well experience similar problems.

amounts to the same question: are you doing what you want to do? If you're lucky, or really determined you'll have landed a career in your early adulthood that satisfies you; or you'll have set out to explore and experiment with a variety of jobs until you found one that suited you. For most people, though, this happens only in part or not all, and the general changes that crop up at midlife give them the opportunity to think about what they really want to do.

Sometimes the onset of midlife coincides with extra work challenges and stress, and you get to the point where you wonder if it's worth it, working in this way. In fact most careers carry various degrees of stress or pressure over and above the nature of work demands; there can be conflicts of personality between you and your colleagues or between you and your boss, and you can be drawn into all sorts of internal power struggles. Some careers demand enormous amounts of time and commitment which can make it very hard for the individual to think about anything else but the job. And many women these days hold down demanding jobs during the day only to go home to take up their second careers, running the home and family. This kind of situation can often be an unbearable and unrecognized workload on the person concerned. Thus, a woman with a career may feel that she cannot give as much as she may want to her career and wonder if it's worth the effort. By the same token family changes at midlife may mean that she can give more of herself to her career.

Often at midlife you may be tempted to wonder if this is really what you had hoped for out of a career. Frequently these events act as a catalyst forcing you to re-think what it is that you want to do, both in the sense of actual career choice and in the sense of whether you want to work at all in the way that you have in the past.

Self-fulfilment

There is a key developmental issue involved here that makes facing up to these questions a matter of personal importance. Remember earlier in this chapter we talked about children being raised to plan a career as a way of thinking about getting involved with the Big World? Well, this process plays a vital role in the development of our personalities in that we all need to feel that we can cope in the world, that we have a role to

---

Forget absenteeism – now it's presenteeism

Remember absenteeism, when people stayed away from work? Well, many people nowadays have to be at work so much of the time and have to work so hard that they find it difficult to take holidays or breaks. Part of this is due to contemporary economic pressures; with firms cutting down on their staff, there are fewer people having to do more work. Part of it is also due to prestige; you have to put in more hours just to stay on top, to remain competitive. In Japan where working hard is a powerful cultural ethic this has got to the point where doctors have had to recognize a new category of industrial accident: death from overwork.

play. It's more than a matter of being able to survive economically; it also helps us to survive psychologically. We spend the earlier part of our adult lives tackling the economic issues involved and as a result typically neglect the psychological side of the task until we get the opportunity to do so at midlife.

It seems to me that many people reach midlife feeling that they are not in charge of what they're doing, that they are at the mercy of pressures – economic, social or psychological – that restrict them. Many men feel that they are trapped by their career or family responsibilities while many women experience emotional difficulties at midlife due to feelings of unfulfilment and frustration at not being given the opportunity to tackle life's challenges to the full.

Dealing directly with reality in all its complexity is one of the most important challenges we all have to face in life. As we noted earlier, exploring reality ourselves forms a vital part of our development. The difficulty is that the way things are structured in our society, the gender roles we have to play can prevent us from dealing with this full complexity.

Women and self-fulfilment

In our society the tradition of the man devoting himself to his career while the woman devotes herself to the family may still hold, but was all the more defined when most of today's middle-aged people were making their career choices. One result of this is that by and large women frequently find their contact with the world outside the family limited to a narrow set of roles. There has also been very little recognition of the demands and complexities of rearing children and running a home. The male's role has tended to be considered more important, to the extent that even when a woman has a career, she may feel that her husband's should come first.

Women have sometimes had to live through their husbands, who are expected to deal with the 'outside' world and whose experiences of it can often set the scene for the woman's perspective on life. Women may often be barred from directly experiencing the kinds of anxiety and pressure that their husbands have to face and end up playing either a supportive or a critical role without ever having the chance to have a go at the problems themselves.

It's official: taking control of your life is good for you

There is now evidence that people who do not get the chance to get involved in dealing with the broad aspects of life struggle more in coping with stress compared to people who do get involved. Coping with stress is not an easy matter anyway, but it's made a good deal worse if you feel that you are not in control over what is happening to you; it makes you feel helpless and vulnerable. Most of us need to feel in control, or in charge of our lives in order to feel confident and sure of ourselves. Feeling that you are at the mercy of outside forces, other people or pressures that you can do nothing about, is often cited as one of the main causes of long-term depressive illnesses and a variety of other health-related disorders.

There is a deeper social issue here. Men are perhaps reared to deal with reality in a way that women are not. They have the opportunity for action and control through their careers, while women are more often their supporters, living relatively protected lives in the background.

What effect can this have? What can this do to your confidence and feeling of being worth something? Can you remember as a teenager how frustrating it was always being dismissed as irrelevant simply because you were thought to be too young to know anything? Well, this form of humiliation seems to me to be the lot of a good number of women long after they've grown out of their teens.

Men and self-fulfilment

There is another side to this story. Just as society inhibits a woman's need to explore her own power and abilities in the world, so society may restrict the opportunity men have of experiencing important aspects of reality. Modern working pressures often ensure that there is little time for and recognition of a man's need to experience parenting and home-building. Just as women often have to deal with the outside world through the medium of their husbands' personalities, so men often have to experience their families at second-hand through the medium of their wives' personalities. Some men, but by no means all, reach midlife feeling that they are 'not known' as people outside their roles as providers, and they resent the way they have had to force their personalities into preordained patterns.

THINGS TO DO: FIVE STEPS TO A FULFILLING JOB

Overall there is a growing awareness of the way we are all to some extent pressured into playing roles that may not challenge us fully as people. More and more people today complain that they are not known fully, that they don't get the chance to know themselves, that career decisions taken in their early twenties do not always fulfil their needs once they reach midlife.

The challenge is to find out what it is that you want to do and then find a way of doing it. Like all the other challenges that come up during midlife we have to take care to proceed with caution. It's no good rebelling in one impulsive act only to discover that you've jumped from the frying pan into the fire. Like all acts of change, it's important to think things through first and to try to get at the deeper issues involved. Ask yourself the following questions before you make a move:

1 *Why are you in your career?*
Before anything else can happen you need to be clear about why you are in your current career. Did you choose your career? Did you have it chosen for you? Or did you just drift into it? Many people do just drift into careers as a way of making money, or make their choice to please others. If you're satisfied with the way things have turned out, don't change. But if you're not, it would help to sort out your feelings clearly first; try to establish just what it is that you do and don't like about your job. Careers often contain their own intrinsic satisfaction which comes from the pleasure of doing a job – any job – well; or just the act of working with other people in a team can be enormously rewarding. Likewise you might like the idea of the career you've chosen but

not do it very well or not like working with people. It's important to get this clear in your own mind first before you consider other issues. Careers are big experiences (not just jobs) and sometimes it may be a matter of adding things to the job rather than changing the job.

2 *What pressures are you under?*

There are enormous social pressures and anxieties that we face in life, and none more so than over the matter of earning money. If you have a family or dependants to support, you will have to think very carefully about your economic survival, and this will be perhaps the most powerful single pressure locking you in place.

If you're under different sorts of pressure, things may be easier. If you feel pressured for example by what important people in your life will think of you if you change career, or start a career, then you have more room to move. You can try examining why you allow yourself to be so pressured and try to find a solution that satisfies you. One problem that people sometimes face – especially women – is that they don't give enough importance to their own need as an individual to work and do something that they really want to do. They weigh up the pressures and may feel that their own needs are too unimportant to be worth doing something about: but the thing about being in midlife is that you *should be* thinking about yourself – it really matters that you find your own way.

Whatever the case, you have to protect your ability to survive economically and emotionally before you make a change. You have to weigh up your wants and needs: not an easy task but one which can be done if you and the important people in your life are prepared to face the issues and to consider alternatives. One alternative is to try work- or role-sharing with your partner which a number of people are trying today, either out of choice or economic necessity.

3 *Is the job the problem?*

You have to be careful to work out what it is about your job that you don't like. If you don't like the pressure and stress, it's of little use doing something else which also involves pressure and stress. By the same token, if you've previously poured yourself into your career role and now

---

The mouse that roared

Sara was a mousy, shy, but intelligent sort of person. Throughout her life she had fitted into the world in a quiet, unfussy way. She wasn't very assertive and had never been troubled by her life, never complained. She was happily married and had two children. A life of quiet contentment. Then it so happened that when she was in her early forties her husband needed someone to run part of their business temporarily. She gladly helped out. It turned out that she was brilliant at what she did. She blossomed and changed completely. She was still the same shy, self-effacing person but now she was alive, active and driven.

At the end of the temporary period her husband tried to get her to give it up. But Sara had found herself and she wasn't going to give it up for anyone. She threatened to break up her marriage if her husband stopped her working, and to prove her point she moved out for a couple of weeks. Eventually he gave in and today she has her own division, a seat on the board and she is still happily married. The funny thing is that she had no idea all this was inside her; she had always considered herself to be entirely happy to leave the work to her husband.

---

want to do things differently and try to explore yourself, you need to have a good look at what's involved before you devote yourself to something else.

Maybe you don't like the people you work with? Do you know why? Is it them or don't you fit in? Some people don't like working with others, they prefer to work alone. Is this you? Sometimes it's not so much a question of a career change but of reorganizing and re-thinking how you work: same job, different arrangement.

4 *Have you taken a good hard look at what you want to do?*
Finding career satisfaction in life is a tough task. Ideally you need to try different things out when you can so that you've

Debbie

Debbie had always poured herself into whatever she did and always complained of the stress involved. She had been a committed housewife and then after her children had grown up she went back to work, where she poured herself into her new task as a nurse. After two years she was back complaining and contemplating another career change. So I asked Debbie to stop for a moment and consider what she would do if she didn't have to work, didn't have to have a career. She was dumbfounded: 'I've got to work. I've never thought about not working. What would I do with myself?' she said. I suggested that she needed to spend some time thinking about what she wanted out of her life and her job. Was she happy? Was she fulfilled? A month later she came back bubbling over with ideas: 'I want to do something that I enjoy for me. Everything I've ever done has been for other people. I'd really like to do something like writing or painting so that I can get some satisfaction for myself out of it.'

In true Debbie fashion she poured herself into this new activity. She took art lessons and began to paint. But she was also sensible and kept on working as a nurse in the meantime until she was sure of what she wanted to do. Today she has, I think, found an ideal compromise. She is an art teacher – doing something for herself while at the same time doing something for other people. More important, I haven't heard her complain for over two years, so I think she's happy.

an idea of what is really involved. What often happens is people give up their existing careers for an ideal or fantasy which then turns out to be not so fantastic. I've known so many people who've thrown up everything to get involved in farming or some other back-to-nature activity only to find that the hours you have to put in leave you precious little time for yourself. I know of men who've swapped roles with their partners because they wanted to be at home and ended up hating the mundanity of it.

At the simplest level, it's worth finding out as much as you can about a potential new career. You'd think this would be an automatic task but so few people do it properly. If they are idealistic about their dreams they often go through the motions about making inquiries but somehow manage to systematically ignore what doesn't fit into the dream.

5 *Are there other ways of getting what you want?*
Again, like the other midlife challenges we have discussed, so much of our own personality and elements of our dream-maps are tied up with our careers. Be sure that you have explored all the avenues for what you want to do so that when you do change, you actually get somewhere. Sometimes there are other ways of getting what you want which may have little to do with job change. Sometimes you can

---

Back to square one

Tony is a person who had been complaining for years about how frustrated he was with his job (he was an accountant) to the extent that it became an obsession. He was determined to get out of the rat race and move to the country, spend more time with his wife. Eventually when he was middle-aged and his children had left home, he fulfilled his obsession. He hauled his wife off to work a plot of land he'd bought and for a while he was happy. Then he began to think of something else. Perhaps he wasn't exactly cut out for the country? He then became obsessed with moving to the outskirts of his county town and trying his hand at landscape gardening, which he did. At this point he met a young woman, and within six months he'd divorced his wife, moved back to the city he came from and started up as, yes, an accountant again. But now he was quite happy to do so. What had happened to Tony was that he'd used his career as a focus for countless frustrations he felt with his life and particularly with his marriage. He wasn't a particularly insightful fellow and he could have saved himself (and his unfortunate wife) a lot of trouble if he'd tried to think things out first.

do things in your spare time that can help make you more satisfied, sometimes not. But have a look first. The point is that the act of doing something fulfilling is what matters, it doesn't necessarily have to be a formal career.

| THE KEY ISSUE | *Self-knowledge leads to development* |

Ultimately whatever you do will be right for you if you have first recognized that part of what you do will involve exploring yourself carefully as a person as well. You'll then have a much better idea of what you need to do. Lots of people get into careers for reasons that only become clear later, most often during midlife. Take me, for example. I'm a psychologist as I've wanted to be since I was a teenager, but part of the reason I wanted to be one had to do with my own personal needs – I thought I'd find out about people through studying them. This was true up to a point, but in the process I realized that while I ended up knowing a lot about people, I knew very little about myself. I had tried to find myself through my career (many psychologists and psychiatrists have similar motivations). Once I had realized this it followed that I had a lot of work, a lot of real living to do for myself in addition to being a psychologist. Since then I've made many changes, explored other areas, other talents (such as playing in a rock band) and lost a good deal of weight.

It is important that we take control of our lives but this also means taking control of our own individuality and dreams. It also means taking the responsibility for whatever happens. Part of the reason so many of our dreams remain locked in our minds as fantasies, untested in reality, is precisely because they are safer there. It's the act of developing them, fulfilling them, that creates the danger and the excitement.

CHAPTER EIGHT

Getting Healthy, Staying Alive

Most of us reach midlife well aware that the next part of our lives is going to be a lot tougher than the first part. We've usually absorbed the media articles about the risks to health that crop up during midlife and we know something about how potentially disturbing things like ageing and the menopause can be. There is now a vast array of suggested measures available to help us cope: diet, exercise, relaxation, vitamin supplements, bone mass supplements, hormone replacement therapy and so on.

How are we to make sense of all the bewildering and sometimes conflicting information we are given? Can changing your diet, stopping smoking or taking up exercise really save (or at least prolong) your life? And what are the health challenges that are specific to midlife as opposed to life in general? We'll try in this chapter to get to the heart of these issues and hopefully gain a better perspective about what is actually going on healthwise during midlife.

First, though, it helps to have a clear idea about what we are exploring. The life expectancy of people today has increased largely due to advances made in public health policies and medical treatment. However, we still run the risk of disease, and some like cancer and diseases of the heart have now become much more prevalent. Why is this?

Part of the reason is because the effects of these diseases, although present throughout history, tended to be obscured by poor social and economic conditions which saw that people died of ill health long before the chronic diseases set in. Furthermore, we used to think of diseases as being caused by unpleasant foreign entities like bacteria and viruses that made you ill by somehow getting into the body and causing harm. However this is only part of the picture and applies only under certain conditions. As medicine has progressed it has become clear that there is a complex relationship between these foreign entities and the body, and different models have had to be developed to help explain what happens.

The body for example is a willing host to many different kinds of bacteria and viruses and actually needs them to achieve healthy functioning. It is now appreciated that illness is caused as much by changes in the internal state of the body as it is by the presence of foreign entities; that in fact we survive by establishing a healthy balance with the germs that inhabit our bodies. Our immune system for instance needs to have contact with friendly bacteria and viruses in order to manufacture the antibodies needed to survive attacks by more virulent versions. It is now apparent that many of the modern-day health problems we face occur as a result of things we do to ourselves over time which interfere with the normal balance the body has with these foreign entities: for example our eating, sleeping and exercise habits affect the efficiency of our immune systems and vital organs.

What has become clear is that the health risks we face today in midlife arise to an important degree out of the way we have lived our lives and the way we have coped with change, stress and problems long before we get to middle-age. We have seen how who we are affects how we respond to the normal biological changes of midlife; much the same is true about the other health risks we face. What we have to realize is that at midlife there is still time to change, still time to learn better ways of coping so that we can enjoy the future. So much of what we can do is in our own hands.

What then are the health risks that we face as middle-aged people in the late 20th century? Overall we face the same underlying health threats that middle-aged people have always faced: a gradual wearing and tearing of body systems that may make us vulnerable to disease. Women may suffer from the consequences of changes in hormonal levels following the menopause and we all face the increased likelihood of falling victim to diseases such as cancer and heart disease.

In Chapter Two we looked at the hormonal and ageing changes that occur during midlife, so before we look at how to tackle the midlife health issues let's take a brief look at the diseases that occur at or after midlife. As I hope you will see, the survival plan I will be outlining later applies right across the board. It's a plan designed for midlife survival in general but it is especially relevant for people at risk from disease. Knowing your risk status can help give you an idea of what may happen to you and alert you to the kind of steps you have to take.

THE RISKS

Cancer, heart disease and some auto-immune diseases like rheumatoid arthritis are chronic diseases. This means that they involve long-term changes in the body and are the result of several factors coming together slowly over the course of time, often as long as 15 or 20 years. Some forms of these diseases do have a different course; there are, for example, quick-onset fast-spreading cancers that apparently come out of the blue, and there are some heart conditions that suddenly strike without warning. By and large these are relatively rare events. It is much more likely to be the case, certainly for the common cancers and heart conditions, that the processes that cause them build up over years.

Genetic influences

It used to be thought that genetic factors played a large part in these chronic diseases; that if your mother had breast cancer or your father a heart condition this predisposed you to having the same condition. There is evidence for this in some cases but the issue is still under debate; do you inherit a gene, or a vulnerability in your body? Or is it that you inherit a family coping strategy whereby the family milieu in which you are reared teaches you a certain way of coping with stress? Most researchers seem to agree that for most forms of these diseases, the role of inherited factors has to be considered alongside many others.

Heart disease

If we look at coronary heart disease (CHD) for example, it is now thought that several factors interact to set up the conditions for the disease to occur. In addition to the increased risk of getting the disease if your parents had it, you run a greater risk if you are overweight, if your diet is too high in certain kinds of cholesterol and fatty products, and if you smoke. But how you cope with stress is also thought to play a role; several personality characteristics or ways of behaving have been linked to the development of CHD. People who are highly competitive, hostile, impatient, and who use behaviourally explosive mannerisms when they are under pressure are thought to be at risk. The risks increase if these characteristics translate into an over-reactive physiology, that is, if they raise blood pressure or induce hypertension. You probably know someone who does all these things, is always in a hurry, rushes their meals, smokes too much, and goes up in smoke when things don't go their way.

How do these various factors come together to cause CHD? If we simplify the function of the heart and leave aside certain heart diseases that directly affect the structure of the heart, we

---

Men and women at risk

Traditionally men were thought to be more likely than women to get heart attacks with some authors suggesting that this may be partly due to the stresses and pressures of their jobs; in the past men were more likely to hold highly pressured positions than women. But it may also be that women are under-represented in studies since it is now recognized that women's heart diseases have not been as thoroughly studied. CHD is now the most frequent cause of death in American women, and women who have a heart attack are less likely to survive than men. In women, a link has also been found between the experience of stress and the development of CHD; most vulnerable are women who are prone to fits of depression and to panic attacks.

see that the heart needs two things to function properly: adequate blood flow and at a reasonable pressure. We can influence this function by interfering in some way with the blood flow. Think of water running through a pipe. If the pipe has been in use for years, it's very likely that the interior of the pipe will have become coated with layer upon layer of sediment which will interfere with the rate and pressure at which water flows. The human heart works in a very similar fashion and we can interfere with the blood flow in two basic ways: by narrowing or altering the structure of the arteries, and by varying the pressure at which the blood flows.

Hardening of the arteries, arteriosclerosis, is believed to be one of the most important sources of myocardial infarction and angina pectoris, two common heart complaints, and it is believed that elements in our diets and heavy smoking can help to narrow the arteries. Similarly, there are a number of ways in which we can interfere with the pressure at which blood flows. If you have chronic high blood pressure your arterial walls will have to operate at too high a level of pressure for too long and can become damaged. If you have an over-reactive pattern of response to stress this can result in your heart literally not getting enough rest.

Obviously the more risk factors you manifest, the greater the risk. A number of studies have suggested that people who tend to over-react physiologically to stress, are very often also the people likely to be using other high-risk ways of coping with life's pressures. Many highly reactive people for example also use smoking, drinking and overeating to get by. It's this matrix of factors that creates the risk and there is some evidence that these traits are laid down very early, even in childhood; not that this necessarily means there are a lot of junior smokers but rather that there may well be a lot of junior over-reactors in training.

Cancer

Cancer is a disease very different from CHD but its aetiology is similarly complex, although different body systems are involved. Cancer is the general name applied to a range of diseases whose effects are often quite different depending on whereabouts in the body they occur. They do however have a common style of acting, and the best way to think about cancer is to look at this basic pattern of working. A tumour is a neoplasm, which simply means a new growth or a collection of new cells that grow usually in response to damage or invasion by a foreign entity. As such, neoplasms occur all the time in the body as part of the way the body repairs damaged tissue. Normally, after a certain time for repair, the body sends a 'stop' message to the damaged area and the growth stops. In cancer this message for one reason or another doesn't get through, and the cells continue to reproduce. Moreover, the new cells tend to be immature, less competent versions of the old ones. Gradually the malignant (as opposed to benign) tumour takes on more and more of a life of its own, defying the body's own defences, setting up a 'state within a state', if you like.

Malignant tumours can take years to grow to the size at which they can begin to pose a serious threat to life. A lot depends on where they are because a cancer can grow without signs or pain in one area but not in others. Some people may live to old age, die of some other disease, and only at autopsy is it discovered that they also had cancer.

Cancer does its damage by its ability to spread; as it grows it invades neighbourhood areas and this is when problems start. As it spreads it eats into surrounding normal tissue or organs, eventually destroying them. If a cancer is near to lymph nodes of the body's immune system, the tumour can get into the blood stream and spread to vital organs such as the liver or the brain, a process called metastasis.

Most of the common cancers are started by some external agent that does the initial damage or causes the initial irritation or inflammation. And it is these agents, or carcinogens, that have been the focus of media attention which I think has helped to make the public's understanding of cancer too simplistic. Thus, you will have heard of the links between smoking and cancer, the links between dietary carcinogens and cancer, and the links between excessive exposure to sunlight and the development of skin cancer. But this is only part of the picture. From what we know of how cancer operates it seems clear that apart from a carcinogen to start the ball rolling, whether or not a cancer develops depends on a range of other, equally important factors. Of these perhaps the most important is how efficiently the body's immune system can cope with the carcinogens to which it is exposed. There are many naturally occurring carcinogens and we are all routinely exposed to any number of them, but only a minority of us develop cancer.

The immune system is the body system that is most involved with coping with damage and the presence of foreign entities in the body. It is the immune system that organizes cell repair, fights infections and germs. It is also through the body's immune system that cancer spreads, and many researchers think that this is at least partly because the cancer overwhelms the local immune system and develops an auto-immune state within the body, subverting aspects of the immune system to its own order (a very similar thing happens in AIDS).

In recent years a great deal has been discovered about how the immune system works, and it is now clear that its efficiency can vary markedly over time. Not only does the system fluctuate during the day, and from day to day, but tobacco smoke, alcohol, even coffee consumption have been shown to reduce immune efficiency in some people. The immune system is also very vulnerable to stressed body states, especially certain kinds of emotional distress. Chronic anxiety, depression and tension can reduce the efficiency of the immune response, and it appears that this is one of the ways that cancers can develop and grow in the body: a stressed person's immune system may not function well enough to eradicate or stop the growth early on. Again, as with heart disease, cancer seems to be caused by the synergistic interaction of a range of factors; like a traffic accident, it takes a whole set of interconnected circumstances to occur in sequence for the accident to happen. Let's also not forget the time element: we're not talking about sudden-onset disease here, but about systems that are set up over a long period of time – so much so that they've become habitual, things you maybe have taught your body to accept without question.

THE SURVIVAL PLAN

Just as how you cope as an individual can have an effect on the way you experience the hormonal and ageing changes of midlife, so the same factors play a part in helping to determine whether or not you are at risk from disease during midlife. As we have seen, we learn our coping behaviours as we grow up, and some of the ways we cope can have bad consequences for

Personalities at risk

The difficulty is that when you are stressed or upset, you tend also to eat unthinkingly, to drink and smoke excessively, and generally lose touch with your body. This is an important point because some doctors believe that in such a state of mind, people are not focused enough on their own body states so they ignore or over-ride early signs of discomfort or damage. You are too involved in other things to care properly for yourself. A number of researchers believe that there are certain kinds of personality traits and states that are associated with chronically lowered levels of immune system functioning. Such people tend to have difficulty coping with stress and with emotions. It seems also that stressful interpersonal relationships tend to lower immune efficiency in the participants more than other forms of stress do, and more so in people who are over-dependent on their relationships and who have trouble establishing their own autonomy. It's as if they focus all their energies on the relationship and not enough on themselves.

our bodies; we can chose to engage in behaviours that expose us to risk (like smoking) and we can expose our bodies to such tension that they become vulnerable to disease.

Just as there is no one single cause of the health problems we face, so there is no one single solution: remedies that encourage you to believe that you will solve your health problems by following one single course of action, be it a diet, a pill or act of faith, miss the point. It's not a question of its being all in the mind or all in the body. The health challenges we face are complex psychosomatic issues. More important, most of the midlife health risks come out of the same psychosomatic milieu: a failure to take proper care of our bodies and a failure to cope in ways that help us better to survive.

We all know that we should try to stay healthy, but why don't we? What stops us from thinking about the health risks and caring for our bodies? What stops us from learning to cope better? These questions take us to the core of the health issue.

One thing leads to another

There is evidence that the people most at risk from chronic diseases are often hostile, over-reactive individuals who cope with stress by inwardly churning up without being able to express their distress other than through their bad habits. Research into the role that hostility plays in disease shows that hostile people are at increased risk from both cancer and heart disease, and are more likely to smoke and over-indulge in eating and drinking than calmer people. It doesn't stop there; smokers are statistically more accident prone and more likely to die violent deaths than non-smokers. There is evidence too that smokers eat less healthy diets than non-smokers. It's no good just stopping the bad habit, you have to get at the root cause inside you and change thoroughly. Fortunately every little step you take to sort yourself out has subtle knock-on effects throughout your body.

If we look at the research on people who are most likely to live long, healthy lives and to survive things like heart attacks and cancer, we see that time and again health and survival is associated with an ability to be autonomous, to be your own person, to take control of your own life, to be independent and self-caring, and to have a high degree of body awareness. In other words, survivors have an ability to be individuals in the sense that we have been discussing in this book. It's no accident that the survivors in life are often those who have been able to channel their anger and frustration into looking after their own bodies – even if this does sometimes make them seem cantankerous and wilful. They take their frustrations and make them work for them instead of turning them against themselves and messing up their bodies. In short they rebel more constructively than the average person does. They take responsibility for their own survival while other people may be too busy, too stuck in their old ways of doing things to bother to change.

This fits in very well with the general thesis of this book, namely that midlife offers you one of your last chances in life to get your act together and to develop this sense of who you are, to get in touch with the inner person if you like. And for many people when it comes to health matters, the key is learning how to rebel against your own bad habits and learning instead how to cope constructively.

The five steps to survival

There are five basic steps you need to take in order to change your coping patterns, and they can be applied to any health challenge that you face.

1 *Decide what you want to do*
  This is the hard part. You're middle-aged, you've got years left; how do you want to proceed? Do you want to stay dependent on crutches of one kind or another (drugs – prescription or otherwise – alcohol, tobacco, food) for the rest of your life, or do you want to enjoy your body and mind, learn to get the most out of who you are? Do you want to be carried into old age or are you going to make it under your own steam? Or are you too busy, too pressured, to get involved in mundane things like caring for yourself? You have to make a choice, and you have to make it now.

A tough decision

Bill was a middle-aged architect who was diagnosed with cancer out of the blue and given six months to live. There was so little hope that his doctor told Bill to make out a will and wait. Bill decided to take matters into his own hands; he read as much as he could about cancer and realized that his only hope lay in changing how he lived. So he did. He took up yoga, fulfilled a life-long ambition to take a holiday in India, and did everything he could to get fit and healthy in body and mind. He wanted to make the best use of what little time he had left. During the process he lost his wife (who divorced him) and alienated his family (who thought he'd flipped). He did however live. When he died, it was from heart failure, not cancer. And it was at the age of 85.

2 *Get information*

Most people simply don't know enough about the issues involved in coping. You have to get information. You should find out what your specific risks are, and what can be done about them. People who survive or who cope well are usually well-informed; they know the name of the enemy. This helps them get involved in the process of looking after themselves. Too many people simply don't want to know – it helps them to keep their heads in the sand and pretend that bad things will never happen to them.

You also have to find out what is involved psychologically and emotionally in changing how you cope. Many people, when they think about their health at all, want easy, quick solutions that won't take too much time or effort. If there was a pill for good health it would be a bestseller. When you change, you have to do so thoroughly, and this to some extent will mean changing who you are, which will have effects on your life in general, including your relationships with those around you. People shrink from the thought of this, which is a great pity; getting accurate information about what is really involved (as opposed to what you *dread* is involved) will soon show you that in choosing to change you are choosing to improve the *quality* of the life you lead. I won't pretend that changing is easy, but if you value intimacy, good friendships, contact with people, getting to know yourself and fulfilling your dreams, or if you just want to enjoy life and survive, then take yourself and these issues seriously.

3 *Get back to your basic rhythms*

The human body can take a lot of abuse. If you smoke too much, don't eat or drink properly, if you don't exercise or sleep properly, it's very unlikely that you'll fall ill – not straight away, anyway. And this is part of the problem; because our bodies can absorb so much, we find it easy to change it slowly. It is these subtle changes that catch up with us in midlife.

There are basic human body rhythms that we are born with; basic rest/activity cycles that help to keep our bodies in a state of homeostasis. You need to rest after exerting yourself, to exercise when you're feeling stiff and lazy. You need to eat when you're hungry and stop eating when you've had enough and so on. As young children we do these things

---

Get your body working for you instead of against you

Our bodies are sometimes fickle things and they can sometimes work against us. Take what the body does with smoking and you'll see how easy it is to condition the body to accept abuse. Most people don't automatically like smoking – it produces a lot of unpleasant body sensations – but we persist with it because it serves another, more pressing function; it helps us to cope with social anxiety and other kinds of stress. When we want to change we find that the body resists it because it's learnt to depend on it. Insomnia and other poor sleeping habits develop in the same way. People get into bad sleep habits usually because they are preoccupied with other matters. They over-ride their natural rhythms and then find that their bodies have forgotten how to sleep properly. It's easy to teach the body new tricks and once it's learnt them, it helps maintain them by its own responses; when you want to stop or change, you can't because your body fights it.

---

naturally. As we grow up we learn that we can abuse our bodies if we want to without ill effect, and gradually most of us in one way or another or at one time or another allow ourselves to over-ride our basic rhythms. Some of us do it too much and we gradually and systematically establish different rhythms for ourselves that go against our body's natural rhythms.

There are many reasons why we learn to ignore our basic body rhythms but mostly we do so as a part of the way we cope with stress and how we rebel against frustration with our lives. Rebelling and coping with stress go hand in hand; rebellion, as we've seen, is a reaction to things being less than we want, less than perfect, less than we've dreamed. You react by using a harmful stress-coping pattern; the stress doesn't go away so you push the habit even harder as a means of expressing anger and rebellion at the fact that you can't get rid of the problem.

Remember we are talking about long-established ways of

Why basic rhythms are important

Animals in the wild are fit, sleek and smart. This is the natural state, this is what happens when basic rhythms are properly attended to. Did you ever see an over-weight, sluggish chimpanzee suffering headaches or insomnia? I mention chimpanzees because genetically they are almost the same as humans (about 98% similar). The only animals with health problems similar to our own are our pets. This should tell us something about why basic rhythms are important:

- *Weight and intake control*: If you over- or under-eat you won't be fit enough to stay physically mobile. You won't have stamina to cope with challenges, or be properly focused on the challenges in your life – you'll be too busy worrying about your diet or what you're going to eat next. Plus, you can create a range of problems (like indigestion, bad toilet habits, skin problems) to side-track you from the main health tasks you face.
- *Sleep*: How people get by without sleeping properly eludes me. Your body not only needs sleep to rest but dreaming helps your mind tackle problems and sort things out for you without outside interference. Sleep is still the best medicine for most body ailments and stress.
- *Proper relaxation*: If you don't give your body and mind natural breaks, you stop if from completing a recuperation cycle. If you use drugs of any kind to relax you (including alcohol), do so minimally: be sure that a large portion of your rest time is natural rather than chemically induced. Remember, relaxation means rest and change, not just sleep. Doing something different forces you to use other parts of your body and mind.
- *Activity*: The body and mind need to be used to stay healthy. Fitness isn't just a matter of looking good – it does your body good too. Using your mind, keeping your skills alive, staying in touch with your emotions and exploring new ones is what your mind does best.

coping, not about how we cope with an occasional upset. There are many ordinary life crises that can cause specific, here-and-now stress: death, illness, divorce or changing jobs are all stressful events and we sometimes react to them in harmful ways for a short time until we get back on our feet again. We all do this, it is part of growing up; we need outlets for our upset and for our frustration. If we keep it all in for too long though it damages our ability to recover our natural habits and rhythms so that this stress-coping pattern becomes the 'normal' pattern a person uses.

The trouble is that as we pass through adulthood we forget what these patterns are there for; we get lost in coping with our lives and we 'solidify' our unhealthy coping patterns. By the time we reach midlife most of us have forgotten our natural patterns and some of us have even lost track of what we were rebelling about in the first place.

Re-establishing basic body rhythms is absolutely essential; they give our bodies the ability to fight. But more is involved; as we regain contact with our bodies so we regain contact with the emotional problems that lie underneath them. This emotional layer is the gold that lies buried inside the bad habits and is the material we can work with to change our lives. If you find you can't regain your natural rhythms in any area, it usually means you've come up against an emotional problem you need to work at.

4 *Find yourself*

It's not just a matter of giving up smoking or drinking, or losing weight – these help to start the ball rolling but we need to appreciate that part of the task of establishing our survival skills involves looking at the psychological and emotional reasons behind our bad habits and changing these as well as the habits.

What this means in effect is re-examining the way we have learnt to cope with the frustrations of life; in other words, we need to look at our patterns of rebellion and coping. I spend a lot of my time trying to teach people new ways of rebelling, new ways of coping with their frustrations to give their bodies a chance to recover healthy rhythms before disease strikes. The task is to mobilize all that rebellious energy that people pour into bad habits and make it work for them, to put them in touch with the part of their personalities that wants to do things for itself.

Do the job properly

When Roger, a 50 year-old professional man, had a minor heart attack he took all the right precautions to make sure he wouldn't have another one. He stopped smoking, went on a special diet, took up golf, got more sleep, lost weight, stopped drinking and reduced his workload. He followed all the correct steps except one. He did nothing about how he lived emotionally. A hard and driven man, Roger suffered enormously from stress and tension. He was almost permanently anxious and worried abut his family, about achieving his goals in life. He over-reacted with intense irritability and hostility to even minor stresses and strains. You should have seen him in a traffic jam! Asked to learn to relax more and find better ways of expressing his pent-up emotions, he laughed and ridiculed the idea. Sadly he died about two years later – from a heart attack.

I try to get people not just to stop their bad forms of rebelling, but to find out first what is going on behind them, inside their minds, so that the meaning of their habits becomes clear and they can then try to find better ways of achieving their aims. There is always something meaningful behind our acts of rebellion; trying to crush them or block them out doesn't help. You have to find out what they are saying about you first: they give us vital clues about what is going on and what can be done. And don't forget, this applies to bad emotional habits as much as to habits like smoking. As you'll have seen from the section on heart disease, getting angry and irritable in controlled, inner ways can be as harmful as eating the wrong kind of margarine.

I speak from experience. During the early days of my midlife period, after years spent behind a desk, I took up tennis. It was humiliating. You know how it is, so long as you're not actually facing the challenge you harbour fantasies of what you were like the last time you learnt something new – ie when you were 18. And then you try it and you feel your age; your reaction times for example are on a par with your granny's. I discovered though that nothing

brought me more in touch with my real feelings; losing yet
another tennis game to a budding nine-year old seemed to
bring all my frustrations out like nothing else did. I coped
by being calm, controlled on the outside while wanting to
break down and howl on the inside. One day my coach took
me aside and suggested I learn to howl with frustration or
throw my racket around. I was surprised but it worked
wonders for me and I learned three important things. First,
there was unfinished emotional business inside me; I had
forgotten how to learn, how to go through the experience of
trial and error. Second it brought me closer to my emotional
state and I realized that there were things in me and my life
I needed to change. Third, I knew I'd never make it to
Wimbledon!

As you try to get back to your basic rhythms you might
find that there are problems or difficulties that you can't
manage on your own. Get help, either from friends or
professionals.

5 *Take care of yourself*

So you've got all the information, you're ready to go. Now
do it. I mean *really* do it. Too many people dabble in this
area; they make countless starts and never push beyond a
certain point – usually the point at which real change will
be achieved. They are like health dilettantes, playing with
their lives. Get used to the idea that it is your life you are
saving and that it is important. Start listening to your body
and your feelings. Make your dreams work.

The hardest acts of caring are those that we perform for
ourselves; it is so easy to downgrade our own value and
worth and our own needs in favour of conventional pressures, conventional explanations and remedies. You feel
guilty if you give less to your kids or your partner than you
do yourself.

To meet your responsibilities to yourself and to others
you have to develop a strong sense of proportion, which
means that you have to be really thoughtful and take your
own needs in hand. Find a balance between the various
commitments and pressures you have in your life and your
need to look after yourself.

In changing how you cope, you may run into conflicts
with those around you – think of what happens when

The good health check list

- *Don't over-expose your body to potentially harmful substances*: it's no good thinking you can live in a totally safe world: nearly all that we come into contact with has the potential to cause harm – food, alcohol, tobacco smoke, sunlight – but only if overdone. Learn to be moderate.
- *Don't ignore body discomfort*: your body will warn you when it's overtaxed or stressed; insomnia, headaches, constipation, indigestion, breathlessness, dizziness, repeated infections, some skin disorders, loss of appetite, insatiable hunger – they are all telling you to stop, give your body a rest and find out what's wrong.
- *Don't ignore your emotions*: emotions tell us what is going on inside us and they are usually clues or impulses that should direct us into taking steps to relieve or fulfil what we feel. Fulfil your emotions healthily by allowing your body's natural cycle to operate. If you're upset, for example, you should cry, get comfort, and so on with someone you feel safe with. This helps your body and gives you time to think and sort things out. Then get back on your feet. Don't burn and fret and smoulder inside – do something constructive about it. This is why people with good relationships survive – there is more real healthy comfort in being held and touched than in any number of cheeseburgers, bottles of wine or packets of cigarettes.
- *Don't make excuses*: take time to attend to yourself. Most people dig up countless excuses as to why they can't do what they have to do. Think of it as an investment.
- *Don't give up*: if it feels like too much of a struggle at first, don't worry – you've got lots of time. And it takes time.

people stop smoking – but this is what you need to do, these conflicts contain the issues that you need to tackle. And this is where healthy rebellion comes in. You may find yourself having to rebel against some of the pressures on you. Healthy rebellion takes courage because you have to fight against the tendency to give in to the pressures around you and the tendency to use your old, harmful patterns of coping.

Ultimately, though, you are more likely to find that you are your own worst enemy, that your biggest battle will be against your old habits. You will have to rebel against parts of yourself.

| THE KEY ISSUE | *Survival is control* |

It's your life, your choice. If you want to get the most out of life you have to take control of what's happening to you. A large part of this lies in taking control of your health and your body. It's not enough to be a coping, capable, controlling person in your life in general if at the same time you're a wimp when it comes to looking after yourself.

You're middle-aged, it's time to give a thought to your survival. Every little bit helps; it need not be all uphill. Don't forget: our bad habits are clues to what's going on inside us; they point to where we don't cope, and these areas can be worked on. Don't be fatalistic; our bad habits don't automatically make us candidates for cancer or a heart attack. We all to some degree engage in poor health habits; overall the percentage of people who actually get cancer or heart disease is relatively small compared to those who don't.

Your bad habits may restrict what you can get out of life and make you vulnerable to minor illnesses. They won't necessarily make you ill, just make it more likely that you'll need a walking-stick sooner than a healthier person. What is likely to increase the risk though is if your bad habits are part of a deeply-rooted pattern of coping with life's trials and frustrations; in other words, if you feel chronically stressed, pressured or tense and if your bad habits have become as natural to you as breathing.

It's a matter of degree; the more you feel stressed, the more often you are in a state of turmoil inside, the higher the risks. Most of us at least have periods of calm, when we put aside our bad habits and try to get back to our basic rhythms. It's when there is no release from stress and strain that the risks increase significantly.

CHAPTER 9

A Last Word

We can see now just why midlife is such an important time. While life may not begin at 40, it certainly is the case that individual circumstances begin to change at around that time. Of course how you live life thereafter may very well change depending on how you cope with whatever comes up. And in fact a lot does come up: we change biologically, our emotions and our needs may change and there may be changes in our relationships, in our families and in our careers. Whoever said that middle-age was a time of quiet contentment and stability?

Midlife is overflowing with challenges, all of them emerging from the changes that occur. How we cope with these changes is what really matters and can make the difference between enjoying the new-found freedom of opportunity for individual development and growth or floundering in a sea of fear and anxiety. The key lies in trying to be clear about the nature of these changes; people can cope with change if they can see what is going on and see what has to be done. Change becomes fearsome when it is shrouded in mystery and uncertainty.

What I have attempted to do in this book is to explore what happens during midlife so that the various contexts in which the changes occur is made clear. As I hope you will have gathered by now, midlife is an important development stage in life and not just a brief interlude before old age. The changes of midlife give you the chance to do things for yourself, to come to grips with who you are as a person and with what you want to get out of life. The choice is yours: you can become an individual and develop whatever potential you have as an autonomous, independent entity; you can remain trapped in the roles and dependencies that have worked for you in the past, or you can find new compromises incorporating a balance between the old you and the new you.

What should be clear is that how you cope with the challenges of midlife will affect what happens to you in the future. Sooner or later you will have to come to terms with the ultimate biological change, and it makes a lot of sense to use the opportunities that midlife offers to ensure you don't reach the end of your life feeling that you have wasted your time and effort.

You also owe it to yourself to perhaps think about doing a little constructive rebellion as so many middle-aged people are doing these days. Break the mould, do some thinking, open yourself up to yourself and to others. Take on the challenges. Being middle-aged really does mean that you have reached the middle of your life; there's lots more living to come.

There are two points I would like to make in conclusion. It seems to me that one of the most crucial things that middle-aged people are rebelling against today is the unfortunate tendency towards 'youthism' in our society. Midlifers are tired of being thought of as old and staid. When they rebel by trying new things, they are rebelling against a society that has a natural tendency to mock and denigrate middle-aged people attempting things only young people are thought capable of getting away with. They are also rebelling against their own fear of making fools of themselves, against their own self-consciousness. Traditional attitudes take a long time to die out and I feel sure that in the future it will become much more acceptable for midlifers to engage in the kind of rebellions that will help to make them happier and more fulfilled as individuals. In time I think we will arrive at a better definition of maturity than we have now.

The second point concerns relationships. You will have noticed that in each of the areas we have discussed, how you cope depends to a large extent on the kind of relationships you have. Whether it is coping with biological change, health challenges, changes in the family and careers, the challenges that arise are mediated through relationships, with partners, children, parents and friends. Typically our relationships can help or hinder us as we try to adjust, none more so than our intimate relationships. With support we can achieve anything, without it we struggle. I believe that as a society we have only just begun to understand the potential that lies in relationships, and in many ways we have only just started the process of finding out what good personal relationships could be about. Contemporary midlifers, I think, are breaking new ground in this respect and I feel sure that relationships will become the new frontier for exploration and growth in the near future.

Selected Bibliography

The following are some of the more important references I used in the preparation for this book. Those marked with an asterisk I would recommend if you want to read further.

Anderson, M (ed), *Sociology of the Family*, Penguin, Harmondsworth, 1982

Argyle, M and Henderson, M, *The Anatomy of Relationships*, Penguin, Harmondsworth, 1985

Ballinger, C B, 'Psychiatric Aspects of the Menopause', *British Journal of Psychiatry*, Vol 56, pp 773–787, 1990

Berry, D S and Pennebaker, J W, 'Nonverbal and Verbal Emotional Expression and Health', *Psychotherapy & Psychosomatics*, Vol 59, pp 11–19, 1993

Cooke, D, 'Psychosocial Vulnerability to Life Events During the Climacteric', *British Journal of Psychiatry*, Vol 147, pp 71–75, 1985

Christensen, N J and Jensen, E W, 'Effects of Psychosocial Stress and Age on Plasma Norepinephrine Levels: A Review', *Psychosomatic Medicine*, Vol 56, pp 77–83, 1994

Dawkins, R, *The Blind Watchmaker*, Penguin, Harmondsworth, 1991

Deptula, D, Singh, R and Pomara, N, 'Ageing, Emotional States and Memory' *American Journal of Psychiatry*, Vol 150, pp 429–434, 1993

Evans, B, *Life Changes: A Guide to the Menopause, its Effects and Treatment*, Pan, London, 1988*

Fernald, R D, 'Cichlids in Love: What a Fish's Social Caste Tells the Fish's Brain about Sex', *The Sciences*, July–August, pp 27–31, 1993

Finch, C E and Schneider, E L, *Handbook of the Biology of Ageing*, Van Nostrand, New York, 1986

Greer, G, *The Change: Women, Ageing and the Menopause*, Penguin, Harmondsworth, 1992*

Hunter, M S, 'Somatic Experience of the Menopause: A Prospective Study', *Psychosomatic Medicine*, Vol 52, pp 357–367, 1990

International Health Foundation, *A Study of the Attitudes of Women in Belgium, France, Great Britain, Italy and West Germany*, IHF, Brussels, 1969

Jenkins, J H and Karno, M, 'The Meaning of Expressed Emotions: Theoretical Issues Raised by Cross-Cultural Research', *American Journal of Psychiatry*, Vol 149, pp 9–21, 1992

Lock, M, 'Hot Flushes in Cultural Context: The Japanese Case as a Cautionary Tale for the West', in Schönbaum, E (ed), *The Climacteric Hot Flush*, Karger, Basle, pp 40–60, 1991

Lock, M, *Encounters with Ageing: Mythologies of Menopause in Japan and North America*, University of California Press, Los Angeles, 1993

Lock, M, 'The Politics of Midlife and Menopause', in Linenbaum, S and Lock, M (eds), *Knowledge, Power and Practice: The Anthropology of Medicine and Everyday Life*, University of California Press, Los Angeles, pp 330–363, 1993*

Mathews, K A, 'Myths and Realities of the Menopause', *Psychosomatic Medicine*, Vol 54, pp 1–9, 1992

Mathews, K A, 'Influences of Natural Menopause on Psychological Characteristics and Symptoms of Middle-Aged Healthy Women', *Journal of Consulting and Clinical Psychology*, Vol 58, 1990

Schiavi, R C et al, 'Healthy Ageing and Male Sexual Function', *American Journal of Psychiatry*, Vol 147, pp 766–771, 1990

Schiavi, R C et al, 'The Relationship Between Pituitary-Gonadal Function and Sexual Behaviour in Healthy Ageing Men', *Psychosomatic Medicine*, Vol 53, pp 363–374, 1991

Shirer, W L, *Love and Hatred: The Stormy Marriage of Leo and Sonya Tolstoy*, Aurum, London, 1994

Shreeve, C M, *Overcoming the Menopause Naturally*, Arrow, London, 1987

Shuttle, P and Redgrove, P, *The Wise Wound: Myths, Realities and Meanings of Menstruation*, Grove Press, London, 1986*

Stoppard, M, *Menopause*, Dorling Kindersley, London, 1994

Theorell, T, 'Critical Life Changes: A Review', *Psychotherapy & Psychosomatics*, Vol 57, pp 108–117, 1992

Vaughan, D, *Uncoupling: How and Why Relationships Come Apart*, Cedar, London, 1994

Wenger, N K, Speroff, L and Packard, B, 'Cardiovascular Health and Disease in Women', *New England Journal of Medicine*, Vol 329, pp 247–256, 1993

Index